Poems

Francis Scott Key

LITERATURE HOUSE / GREGG PRESS
Upper Saddle River, N. J.

Republished in 1970 by
LITERATURE HOUSE
an imprint of The Gregg Press
121 Pleasant Avenue
Upper Saddle River, N. J. 07458

Standard Book Number—8398-1053-9
Library of Congress Card—79-104503

Printed in United States of America

POEMS.

POEMS

OF THE LATE

FRANCIS S. KEY, ESQ.,

AUTHOR OF
"THE STAR SPANGLED BANNER."

WITH AN INTRODUCTORY LETTER
BY CHIEF JUSTICE TANEY.

NEW YORK:
ROBERT CARTER & BROTHERS,
No. 530 BROADWAY.

1857.

STEREOTYPED BY
THOMAS B. SMITH,
82 & 84 Beekman Street.

S. B. THOMSON,
BINDER,
82 & 84 Beekman St.

PRINTED BY
E. O. JENKINS
24 Frankfort St.

Contents.

PREFACE.

THE poetry which is now given to the public, in the following volume, has long been treasured, amid the circle of private friends, who knew and loved, the late Francis S. Key, Esq. A more gifted intellect, the writer of these lines, has never met with, and hence, has entertained the opinion, that it was due to the "literature of song," and would prove a most acceptable contribution to the limited classic poetry of our country, that the effusions of a mind so pure and beautiful, should go forth, and gratify the general reader.

After several years of respectful solicitation, to those possessing the manuscript, permission to publish it has been obtained, together with a narrative, from the accurate pen of Chief Justice Taney, brother-in-law of Mr. Key, of the circumstances originating and attending, the composition of the national ballad, entitled, "The Star Spangled Banner." As probably few of

those who read and admire, that thrilling effusion, are
acquainted with its history, and as it is desirable to
fix the same, in a more enduring form than the mem-
ory of private friendship, it is believed that it will be
eminently satisfactory, that an opportunity has now
been presented for giving it to the press. The gen-
erous soul of American patriotism will not the less
earnestly value the "Banner," when fully apprized of
the occasion of composing " the ballad."

The piece entitled " the Nobleman's Son, etc.," was
written on the back of a letter, as Mr. Key was return-
ing to Baltimore from professional engagements, in the
Supreme Court, at Washington. The undersigned, de-
sires to express no preference among so much excel-
lence, as appears in Mr. Key's poetry ; but ventures to
ask the reader's eye, for the stanza in this piece descrip-
tive of the scene when the Saviour's power, and the
mother's falling tear, and the abated " fever's rage," are
grouped in a manner so inimitably beautiful. There
are two lines here which may be surpassed by others
in our rich and flowing language, but if so, they have
not yet met the writer's notice.

Throughout the whole of these brief, but touching

compositions, the deep-toned piety, social disposition, and chastened cheerfulness of our lamented friend, are constantly apparent. If anything need be said in the form of a motive for asking permission to give this volume to the public, it must be found in a deep and cherished respect for its author, and the settled conviction that his poems cannot fail to gratify the lover of the pure and beautiful, in every land. Real poetry is a rare birth amid the deformities of a blighted world. When it appears, elevated and warmed by the spirit of our holy religion, no arithmetic can tell its value. It ought not to be locked up in the closet of private friendship, for it belongs to " man."

HENRY V. D. JOHNS.
LANVALE STREET, BALTIMORE,
August, 26th, 1856.

LETTER

FROM

HON. CHIEF JUSTICE TANEY,

NARRATING THE INCIDENTS CONNECTED WITH THE
ORIGIN OF THE SONG

"THE STAR SPANGLED BANNER."

LETTER.

My Dear Sir :—

I promised some time ago to give you
an account of the incidents in the life of Mr. F. S.
Key, which led him to write the "Star Spangled
Banner," and of the circumstances under which it
was written. The song has become a national one,
and will, I think, from its great merit, continue to
be so, especially in Maryland ; and everything
that concerns its author must be a matter of inter-
est to his children and descendants. And I pro-
ceed to fulfill my promise with the more pleasure,
because while the song shows his genius and taste
as a poet, the incidents connected with it, and the
circumstances under which it was written, will
show his character and worth as a man. The
scene he describes, and the warm spirit of patriot-
ism which breathes in the song, were not the off-

spring of mere fancy, or poetic imagination. He describes what he actually saw. And he tells us what he felt while witnessing the conflict, and what he felt when the battle was over, and the victory won by his countrymen. Every word came warm from his heart, and for that reason, even more than from its poetical merit, it never fails to find a response in the hearts of those who listen to it.

You will remember that in 1814, when the song was written, I resided in Frederic, and Mr. Key in Georgetown. You will also recollect, that soon after the British troops retired from Washington, a squadron of the enemy's ships made their way up the Potomac, and appeared before Alexandria, which was compelled to capitulate; and the squadron remained there some days, plundering the town of tobacco, and whatever else they wanted. It was rumored, and believed in Frederic, that a marauding attack of the same character would be made on Washington and Georgetown, before the ships left the river. Mr. Key's family were still in Georgetown. He would not, and indeed could not, with honor, leave the place, while it was threatened by the enemy; for he was a volunteer in the Light Artillery, commanded by Major Peter, which was composed of citizens of the District of Columbia, who had uniformed themselves, and offered their services to the government, and who had been employed in active service from the time the British fleet appeared in the Patuxent preparatory to the movement upon Washington. And Mrs. Key refused to leave home, while Mr. Key was thus daily exposed to danger. Believing, as we did, that an attack would probably be made on Georgetown, we became very anxious about the situation of his family. For if the attack was made, Mr. Key would be with the troops engaged in the defense; and as it was impossible to foresee what would be the issue of the conflict, his family, by remaining in Georgetown, might be placed in great and useless peril. When I speak of *we*, I mean Mr. Key's father and mother, and Mrs. Taney and myself. But it was agreed among us, that I should go to Georgetown, and try to persuade Mrs. Key, to come away with their children, and stay with me or with Mr. Key's father, until the danger was over. When I reached Georgetown, I found the English ships still at Alexandria, and a body of militia encamped in Washington, which had been assembled to defend the city. But it was then believed, from information received, that no attack would be made by the enemy on Washington, or Georgetown; and preparations were making, on our part, to annoy them by batteries on shore, when they descended the river. The knowledge of these preparations probably hastened their departure; and the second or third day after my arrival, the ships were seen moving down the Potomac.

On the evening of the day that the enemy disappeared, Mr. Richard West arrived at Mr. Key's, and told him that after the British army passed through Upper Marlbro', on their return to their ships, and had encamped some miles below the town, a detachment was sent back, which entered Dr. Beanes's house about midnight. compelled him to rise from his bed, and hurried him off to the British camp, hardly allowing him time to put his clothes on ; that he was treated with great harshness, and closely guarded ; and that as soon as his friends were apprized of his situation, they hastened to the head-quarters of the English army to solicit his release, but it was peremptorily refused, and they were not even permitted to see him ; and that he had been carried as a prisoner on board the fleet. And finding their own efforts unavailing, and alarmed for his safety, his friends in and about Marlbro' thought it advisable that Mr. West should hasten to Georgetown, and request Mr. Key to obtain the sanction of the government to his going on board the admiral's ship under a flag of truce, and endeavoring to procure the release of Dr. Beanes, before the fleet sailed. It was then lying at the mouth of the Potomac, and its destination was not at that time known with certainty. Dr. Beanes, as perhaps you know, was the leading physician in Upper Marlbro', and an accomplished scholar and gentleman. He was highly respected

2*

by all who knew him; was the family physician of
Mr. West, and the intimate friend of Mr. Key.
He occupied one of the best houses in Upper Marl-
bro', and lived very handsomely; and his house
was selected for the quarters of Admiral Cock-
burn, and some of the principal officers of the
army, when the British troops encamped at Marl-
bro' on their march to Washington. These officers
were of course furnished with everything that the
house could offer; and they, in return, treated him
with much courtesy, and placed guards around his
grounds and out-houses, to prevent depredations by
their troops.

But on the return of the army to the ships,
after the main body had passed through the town,
stragglers who had left the ranks to plunder, or
from some other motive, made their appearance
from time to time, singly or in small squads; and
Dr. Beanes put himself at the head of a small
body of citizens, to pursue and make prisoners of
them. Information of this proceeding, was, by
some means or other, conveyed to the English

camp; and the detachment of which I have spoken was sent back to release the prisoners, and seize Dr. Beanes. They did not seem to regard him, and certainly did not treat him, as a prisoner of war, but as one who had deceived, and broken his faith to them.

Mr. Key readily agreed to undertake the mission in his favor, and the President promptly gave his sanction to it. Orders were immediately issued to the vessel usually employed as a cartel, in the communications with the fleet in the Chesapeake, to be made ready without delay; and Mr. John S. Skinner, who was agent for the government for flags of truce and exchange of prisoners, and who was well known as such to the officers of the fleet, was directed to accompany Mr. Key. And as soon as the arrangements were made, he hastened to Baltimore, where the vessel was, to embark; and Mrs. Key and the children went with me to Frederic, and thence to his father's on Pipe Creek, where she remained until he returned.

We heard nothing from him, until the enemy

retreated from Baltimore, which, as well as I can now recollect, was a week or ten days after he left us; and we were becoming uneasy about him, when, to our great joy, he made his appearance at my house, on his way to join his family.

He told me that he found the British fleet, at the mouth of the Potomac, preparing for the expedition against Baltimore. He was courteously received by Admiral Cochrane, and the officers of the army, as well as the navy   But when he made known his business, his application was received so coldly, that he feared it would fail. General Ross and Admiral Cockburn—who accompanied the expedition to Washington—particularly the latter, spoke of Dr. Beanes, in very harsh terms, and seemed at first, not disposed to release him. It, however, happened, fortunately, that Mr. Skinner carried letters from the wounded British officers left at Bladensburg ; and in these letters to their friends on board the fleet, they all spoke of the humanity and kindness with which they had been treated, after they had fallen into our hands. And after a good deal of conversation, and strong representations from Mr. Key, as to the character and standing of Dr. Beanes, and of the deep interest which the community in which he lived, took in his fate, General Ross said that Dr. Beanes deserved much more punishment than he had received; but that he felt himself bound to make a return for the kindness which had been shown to his wounded officers, whom he had been compelled to leave at Bladensburg; and upon that ground, and that only, he would release him. But Mr. Key was at the same time informed that neither he, nor any one else, would be permitted to leave the fleet for some days; and must be detained until the attack on Baltimore, which was then about to be made, was over. But he was assured that they would make him and Mr. Skinner, as comfortable as possible, while they detained them. Admiral Cochrane, with whom they dined on the day of their arrival, apologized for not accommodating them in his own ship, saying that it was crowded already with officers of the army; but that they would be well taken care of in the frigate *Surprise*, commanded by his son, Sir Thomas Cochrane. And to this frigate, they were accordingly transferred.

Mr. Key had an interview with Dr. Beanes, before General Ross consented to release him. I do not recollect whether he was on board the admiral's ship, or the *Surprise*, but I believe it was the former. He found him in the forward part of the ship, among the sailors and soldiers; he had not had a change of clothes from the time he was seized; was constantly treated with indignity by those around him, and no officer would speak to him. He was treated as a culprit, and not as a prisoner of war. And this harsh and humiliating treatment continued until he was placed on board the cartel.

Something must have passed, when the officers were quartered at his house, on the march to Washington, which, in the judgment of General Ross, bound him not to take up arms against the English forces, until the troops had re-embarked. It is impossible on any other ground, to account for

the manner in which he was spoken of, and treated.
But whatever General Ross, and the other officers
may have thought, I am quite sure that Dr. Beanes
did not think he was in any way pledged to abstain
from active hostilities against the public enemy.
And when he made prisoners of the stragglers, he
did not consider himself as a prisoner on parole,
nor suppose himself to be violating any obligation
he had incurred. For he was a gentleman of un-
tainted character, and a nice sense of honor, and
incapable of doing anything that could have just-
ified such treatment. Mr. Key imputed the ill-
usage he received to the influence of Admiral
Cockburn, who, it is still remembered, while he
commanded in the Chesapeake, carried on hostili-
ties in a vindictive temper, assailing and plunder-
ing defenceless villages ; or countenancing such
proceedings by those under his command.

Mr. Key and Mr. Skinner continued on board
of the *Surprise*, where they were very kindly
treated by Sir Thomas Cochrane, until the fleet
reached the Patapsco, and preparations were mak-

ing for landing the troops. Admiral Cochrane
then shifted his flag to the frigate, in order that he
might be able to move further up the river, and su-
perintend in person, the attack by water, on the
fort. And Mr. Key and Mr. Skinner were then
sent on board their own vessel, with a guard of sail-
ors, or marines, to prevent them from landing.
They were permitted to take Dr. Beanes with them
and they thought themselves fortunate in being an-
chored in a position which enabled them to see dis-
tinctly the flag of Fort McHenry from the deck
of the vessel. He proceeded then with much ani-
mation to describe the scene on the night of the
bombardment. He and Mr. Skinner remained on
deck during the night, watching every shell, from
the moment it was fired, until it fell, listening with
breathless interest to hear if an explosion followed.
While the bombardment continued, it was sufficient
proof that the fort had not surrendered. But it
suddenly ceased some time before day; and as
they had no communication with any of the ene-
my's ships, they did not know whether the fort had

surrendered, or the attack upon it been abandoned. They paced the deck for the residue of the night in painful suspense, watching with intense anxiety for the return of day, and looking every few minutes at their watches, to see how long they must wait for it; and as soon as it dawned, and before it was light enough to see objects at a distance, their glasses were turned to the fort, uncertain whether they should see there the stars and stripes, or the flag of the enemy. At length the light came, and they saw that " our flag was still there." And as the day advanced, they discovered, from the movements of the boats between the shore and the fleet, that the troops had been roughly handled, and that many wounded men were carried to the ships. At length he was informed that the attack on Baltimore had failed, and the British army was re-embarking, and that he and Mr. Skinner, and Dr. Beanes, would be permitted to leave them, and go where they pleased, as soon as the troops were on board, and the fleet ready to sail.

He then told me that, under the excitement of

3

the time, he had written a song, and handed me a
printed copy of "The Star Spangled Banner."
When I had read it, and expressed my admiration,
I asked him how he found time, in the scenes he
had been passing through, to compose such a song?
He said he commenced it on the deck of their ves-
sel, in the fervor of the moment, when he saw the
enemy hastily retreating to their ships, and looked
at the flag he had watched for so anxiously as the
morning opened; that he had written some lines, or
brief notes that would aid him in calling them to
mind, upon the back of a letter which he happened
to have in his pocket; and for some of the lines, as
he proceeded, he was obliged to rely altogether on
his memory; and that he finished it in the boat on
his way to the shore, and wrote it out as it now
stands, at the hotel, on the night he reached Balti-
more, and immediately after he arrived. He said
that on the next morning, he took it to Judge
Nicholson, to ask him what he thought of it,
that he was so much pleased with it, that he imme-
diately sent it to a printer, and directed copies to
be struck off in hand-bill form; and that he, Mr.

Key, believed it to have been favorably received
by the Baltimore public.

Judge Nicholson and Mr. Key, you know, were
nearly connected by marriage, Mrs. Key and Mrs.
Nicholson being sisters. The Judge was a man of
cultivated taste, had at one time been distinguished
among the leading men in Congress, and was at
the period of which I am speaking the Chief Just-
ice of the Baltimore, and one of the Judges of the
Court of Appeals, of Maryland. Notwithstanding
his judicial character, which exempted him from
military service, he accepted the command of a
volunteer company of artillery. And when the
enemy approached, and an attack on the fort was
expected, he and his company offered their services
to the government, to assist in its defence. They
were accepted, and formed a part of the garrison,
during the bombardment. The Judge had been
relieved from duty, and returned to his family only
the night before Mr. Key showed him his song.
And you may easily imagine the feelings with
which, at such a moment, he read it, and gave it

to the public.   It was, no doubt, as Mr. Key modestly expressed it, favorably received.   In less than an hour after it was placed in the hands of the printer, it was all over town, and hailed with enthusiasm, and took its place at once. as a national song.

I have made this account of " The Star Spangled Banner" longer than I intended, and find that I have introduced incidents and persons outside of the subject I originally contemplated.   But I have felt a melancholy pleasure in recalling events connected, in any degree, with the life of one with whom I was so long and so closely united in friendship and affection; and whom I so much admired for his brilliant genius, and loved for his many virtues.   I am sure, however, that neither you, nor any of his children or descendants, will think the account I have given too long.

With great regard, dear sir,

Your friend truly,

R. B. TANEY

POEMS.

The Star Spangled Banner.

O SAY, can you see, by the dawn's early light,
　What so proudly we hailed, at the twilight's last
　　gleaming ?
Whose broad stripes and bright stars through the
　　perilous fight,
　O'er the ramparts we watched, were so gallantly
　　streaming ;
And the rockets' red glare, the bombs bursting in air,
Gave proof through the night that our flag was
　　still there :
O say, does that Star Spangled Banner yet wave
O'er the land of the free and the home of the brave ?

II.

On that shore, dimly seen through the mists of the
    deep,
    Where the foe's haughty host in dread silence
      reposes,
What is that which the breeze, o'er the towering
    steep,
    As it fitfully blows, now conceals, now discloses ?
Now it catches the gleam of the morning's first beam,
In full glory reflected now shines in the stream :
'Tis the Star Spangled Banner ; O long may it wave
O'er the land of the free and the home of the brave !

III.

And where are the foes who so vauntingly swore
    That the havoc of war, and the battle's confusion,
A home and a country should leave us no more :
    Their blood has washed out their foul footsteps'
      pollution ;

No refuge could save the hireling and slave
From the terror of flight, or the gloom of the grave ;
And the Star Spangled Banner in triumph doth
    wave
O'er the land of the free and the home of the brave !

IV.

O thus be it ever, when freemen shall stand
  Between their loved homes and the war's desola-
    tion ;
Blest with victory and peace, may the heav'n-res-
    cued land
  Praise the Power that hath made and preserved
    us a nation !
Then conquer we must, when our cause it is just,
And this be our motto, " In God is our trust ;"
And the Star Spangled Banner in triumph shall
    wave
O'er the land of the free and the home of the brave !

Song.

WHEN the warrior returns, from the battle afar,
   To the home and the country he nobly defended,
O ! warm be the welcome to gladden his ear,
   And loud be the joy that his perils are ended ;
In the full tide of song let his fame roll along,
To the feast-flowing board let us gratefully throng,
Where, mixed with the olive, the laurel shall wave,
And form a bright wreath for the brows of the brave.

Columbians ! a band of your brothers behold,
   Who claim the reward of your hearts' warm emo-
      tion,
When your cause, when your honor, urged onward
   the bold,
   In vain frowned the desert, in vain raged the ocean:

To a far distant shore, to the battle's wild roar,
They rushed, your fair fame and your rights to
  secure :
Then, mixed with the olive, the laurel shall wave,
And form a bright wreath for the brows of the
  brave.

In the conflict resistless, each toil they endured,
  'Till their foes fled dismayed from the war's des-
    olation :
And pale beamed the Crescent, its splendor obscured
  By the light of the Star Spangled flag of our
    nation.
Where each radiant star gleamed a meteor of war,
And the turbaned heads bowed to its terrible
  glare,
Now, mixed with the olive, the laurel shall wave,
And form a bright wreath for the brows of the
  brave.

Our fathers, who stand on the summit of fame,
   Shall exultingly hear of their sons the proud story :
How their young bosoms glow'd with the patriot flame,
      How they fought, how they fell, in the blaze of
         their glory,
How triumphant they rode o'er the wondering flood,
And stained the blue waters with infidel blood ;
How, mixed with the olive, the laurel did wave,
And formed a bright wreath for the brows of the
      brave.

Then welcome the warrior returned from afar
   To the home and the country he nobly defended ;
Let the thanks due to valor now gladden his ear,
   And loud be the joy that his perils are ended.
In the full tide of song·let his fame roll along,
To the feast-flowing board let us gratefully throng,
Where, mixed with the olive, the laurel shall wave,
And form a bright wreath for the brows of the
      brave.

To My Sister.

I THINK of thee—I feel the glow
Of that warm thought—yet well I know
No verse a brother's love may show,
        My sister !

But ill should I deserve the name
Or warmth divine, that poets claim,
If I for thee no lay could frame,
        My sister !

I think of thee—of those bright hours
Rich in life's first and fairest flowers,
When childhood's gay delights were ours,
        My sister !

4

Those sunny paths were all our own,
And thou and I were there alone,
Each to the other only known,
                    My sister!

In every joy and every care,
We two, and we alone, were there,
The brightness and the gloom to share,
                    My sister!

As changing seasons o'er us flew,
No changes in our love we knew,
And there our hearts together grew,
                    My sister!

And then there came that dreaded day
When I with thee no more must stay,
But to the far school haste away,
                    My sister!

Sad was the parting—sad the days,
And dull the school, and dull the plays,
Ere I again on thee may gaze
              My sister!

But longest days may yet be past,
And cares of school away be cast,
And home and thee be seen at last,
              My sister!

The mountain top, the meadow plain,
The winding creek, the shaded lane,
Shall shine in both our eyes again,
              My sister!

Who then shall first my greeting seek?
Whose warm tear fall upon my cheek?
And tell the joy she cannot speak?
              My sister!

My sister!—those bright days are gone,
And we through life have journeyed on,
With hearts, which still, as then, are one,
                    My sister!

A parting hour again must come,
Again to meet, beyond the tomb—
O! let us then make heaven our home,
                    My sister!

Written To Mr. Key,

BY A LADY IN ALABAMA.

THANKS, gentle fairy—now my album take
And place it on his table ere he wake,
Then whisper, that a maiden all unknown,
Claims from the poet's hand a trifling boon ;
Trifling perchance to him, but oh ! not so
To her whose heart has thrilled long, long ago,
As his inspiring lays came to her ear,
Lending the stranger's name an interest dear.
A timid girl may yet be bold t' admire
The poet's fervor, and the patriot's fire ;
But 'tis not these—though magical their power,
They cannot brighten woman's saddened hour,
And she, the happiest, has saddened hours,
When all life's pathways are bereft of flowers,

4*

And her bowed spirit feels, as felt by thee,
That to " live always" on this earth would be
For her, for all, no happy destiny.

Poet and Patriot ! thou may'st write for fame,
But by a tenderer and holier name
I call thee—Christian !   Write me here one lay,
For me to read and treasure when thou'rt away.

To Miss ———.

AND is it so?—a thousand miles apart,
Has lay of mine e'er touched a gifted heart?
Brightened the eye of beauty? won her smile?
Rich recompense for all the poet's toil.
That fav'ring smile, that brightened eye,
That tells the heart's warm ecstasy,
I have not seen—I may not see—
But, maiden kind! thy gift shall be
A more esteemed and cherished prize
Than fairest smiles or brightest eyes.
And this rich trophy of the poet's power
Shall shine through many a lone and distant hour:
Praise from the fair, howe'er bestowed, we greet;
In words, in looks outspeaking words, tis sweet;

But when it breathes in bright and polished lays
Warm from a kindred heart, this, this is praise.

We are not strangers; in our hearts we own
Chords that must ever beat in unison;
The same touch wakens them: in all we see,
Or hear, or feel, we own a sympathy;
We look where nature's charms in beauty rise,
And the same transport glistens in our eyes.
The joys of others cheer us, and we keep
A ready tear, to weep with those who weep.
'Tis this, that in the impassioned hour,
Gives to the favored bard the power,
As sweetly flows the stream of song,
To bear the raptured soul along,
And make it, captive to his will,
With all his own emotions thrill.
This is a tie that binds us; 'tis the glow,
The " gushing warmth" of heart, that poets know;

We are not strangers—well thy lines impart
The patriot feeling of the poet's heart.
Not even thy praise can make me vainly deem
That 't was the poet's power, and not his theme,
That woke thy young heart's rapture, when from far
His song of vict'ry caught thy fav'ring ear :
That victory was thy country's, and his strain
Was of that starry banner that again
Had waved in triumph on the battle plain,
Yes, though Columbia's land be wide,
Though Chesapeake's broad waters glide
Far distant from the forest shores
Where Alabama's current roars ;
Yet over all this land so fair
Still waves the flag of stripe and star :
Still on the Warrior's banks is seen,
And shines in Coosa's valleys green,
By Alabama's maidens sung
With patriot heart, and tuneful tongue.

Yes, I have looked around me here
And felt I was no foreigner;
Each friendly hand's frank offered clasp
Tells me it is a brother's grasp :
My own I deem these rushing floods,
My own, these wild and waving woods,
And—to a poet, sounds how dear!—
My own song sweetly chanted here.
The joy with which these scenes I view
Tells me this is my country too :
These sunny plains I freely roam;
I am no outcast from a home,
No wanderer on a foreign strand,
"This is my own, my native land."
We are not strangers: still another tie
Binds us more closely, more enduringly;
The poet's heart, though time his verse may save,
Must chill with age, and perish in the grave.
The patriot too must close his watchful eye

Upon the land he loves : his latest sigh
All he has left to give it, ere he die.
But when the Christian faith in power hath spoke
To the bowed heart, and the world's spell is broke,
That heart transformed, a never dying flame
Warms with new energy, above the claim
Of death t' extinguish ;—oh ! if we have felt
This holy influence, and have humbly knelt,
In penitence, for pardon ; sought and found
Peace for each trouble, balm for every wound ;
For us, if Faith this work of love hath done,
Not alike only are our hearts—they're one :
Our joys and sorrows, hopes and fears, the same—
One path our course, one object all our aim ;
Though sundered here, one home at last is given,
Strangers to earth, and fellow heirs of heaven.

Yes ! I will bear thy plausive strain afar,
A light to shine upon the clouds of care,

A flower to cheer me in life's thorny ways,
And I will think of her whose fav'ring lays
Kind greeting gave, and in the heart's best hour
For thee its warmest wishes it shall pour.

And may I hope, when this fair volume brings
Some thought of him who tried to wake the strings
Of his forgotten lyre, at thy command—
Command that warmed his heart, and nerved his
        hand—
Thou wilt for one, who in the world's wild strife
Is doomed to mingle in the storms of life,
Give him the blessing of a Christian's care,
And raise in his defence the shield of prayer.

    TUSCALOOSA, Alabama,
      Dec. 13, 1833.

Written in Miss Triplet's Album.

You ask, fair maiden, for one line, but I must give
    you three,
For a couplet at the least, for the rhyme's sake,
    there must be,
And a Triplet for your name's sake therefore take
    from
                F. S. KEY,

Who hopes that thus, hereafter, whate'er your
    wishes be,
Thrice more and better than you ask may be given
    unto thee!

5

Translation.

THE chiefs were seated, and the soldiers round,
Ranged in due order, filled the extended ground;
When Ajax, master of the sevenfold shield,
In wrath arose, and from the tented field
Turned his stern eye to the Sigeian strand,
And the tall ships fast anchored to the land :
" And is it here, ye Gods," aloud he cried,
" Before this fleet that this great cause is tried?
And is it here that I Ulysses see,
Daring to stand competitor to me ?
Not thus he dared, when Hector's raging hand
Waved here, on high, the desolating brand,
Whose flames I quenched and saved this threatened
strand.

" Full well Ulysses knows 'tis safer far
To wage of empty words, the bloodless war,
Than face a foe in arms ;—nor have I art
For such vain strife, nor hath he hand or heart
For bold exploits : while well-fought fields proclaim
My worth, a smooth, false tongue is all his fame.
Nor need I to the Greeks my deeds display—
Deeds done before their eyes in face of day ;
His, let Ulysses tell, and bring to light
A prowess never shining but by night.

" The baseness of my rival casts a stain
E'en on the glorious prize I seek to gain,
For poor his triumph, whatsoe'er the prize,
Who stoops like me, and with Ulysses vies.
The contest now, however it ensue,
Gives him an honor greater than his due,
And proud enough for him the boast will be,
When vanquished, that he dared contend with me.

" If my own worth suffice not for my claim,
A noble ancestry will lend their fame :
My father, Telamon, who Troy o erthrew
Under great Hercules—whom Colchos knew,
With Jason the renowned.   His sire was he
Who binds the shades below, by his decree,
Where Sisyphus in vain laments his fate,
Beneath the rude rock's ever rolling weight :
Æacus, the mighty Jove's high favors prove
His son ;—and Ajax is the third from Jove.
Nor should this high descent, in this great cause
Avail me, Greeks ! but that Achilles draws
From the same source divine, a kindred name—
Brethren in blood, a brother's arms I claim.

" And shall a base-born stranger dare to place
His hated name among a hero's race ?
Or shall I stand excluded from my right
Who foremost came, unsummoned, to the fight ?

And to a cowardly dissembler yield,
Dragged by device reluctant to the field ?
Pretending madness to conceal his fear,
Till one, more artful, made his fraud appear ?
Shall he, whom skulking then, no arms could please,
Now ask for arms, and dare to ask for these ?—
These, which are doubly mine by right of birth,
And won by valor, as the prize of worth ?

" Ah ! had his madness real been, or feigned
With more successful art !   Had he remained
Safe in his cowardice, nor joined the host
Of Greece and glory on the Trojan coast !
Then never had his counselled deeds of shame
Tarnished the lustre of his country's name,
And Lemnos' shores had never witnessed then
Thy sorrows, Philoctetes ! and our sin,
Where now the lonely rocks and forests hear
The sad and ceaseless cries of thy despair,

2*

Where groans and curses, and the hated name
Of Ithacus, thy miseries proclaim:
Curses and groans that not in vain shall rise,
If there be gods to hear above the skies.
Thus he, our sworn companion in the war,
A wretched outcast from our ranks, afar
On a lone isle, is forced for food t' employ
The weapons destined for the fall of Troy.
Yet still he lives, from further malice free,
Beyond the reach of his base enemy.
Not so another victim: more severe
A fate, O Palamedes! thou must bear;
Death and disgrace Ulysses plots for thee,
The bold detector of his infamy.
Urged by revenge, for this the accuser came,
To pour thy blood upon thy blasted name,
Charged thee with treason, and, in proof, revealed
The gold that in thy tent himself concealed:
Such fame Ulysses' exploits attends,
Thus is he dangerous only to his friends.

And such his aid to Greece : her warriors given
To a foul death or into exile driven.
What though his boasted eloquence exceed
E'en that of Nestor? can e'en that succeed
In justifying the disgraceful flight
That left the aged Nestor in the fight?
He saw the veteran chief, his strength decayed,
And his steed wounded—heard him call for aid,
And basely fled and left him to his foes.
That this is true, brave Diomede well knows,
Who strove, with loud reproaches, to restrain
His flight, and called him back, but called in vain.
But there are gods on high, and they decreed
That he, the aid he would not give, should need.

"Lo now his peril comes : the foe is nigh
He sees, and will not fight and cannot fly.
Will any comrade, if he call, attend?
Will he who basely left, now find, a friend?

He cries for help : I come—I see him lie—
Fear chills his limbs, and quivers in his eye ;
I threw my shield between him and the foe,
And saved his worthless life—a worthless deed, I
      know.
If still thou dar'st with me the contest try,
Return we to that field—there prostrate lie,
With wound, and threatening foe, and wonted fear,
And crouch beneath my shield, and brave me there ;
And when thus rescued, his pretended wound
No hind'rance to the recreant's speed is found ;
And he, who had not strength to stand in fight,
Is soon among the foremost in the flight.
Hector is nigh, in all the rage of war,
The god of battles thundering from his car,
And where he urges on his dread career,
Ulysses well may fly—for heroes fear.
I met him raging with success and wrath ;
Fearless, I threw myself before his path,

Nor was my strength and courage tried in vain:
'T was this right hand that pressed him to the plain;
And when again he came with haughty boast,
And proud defiance of the Grecian host,
And dared the boldest warrior of our band
In single strife to meet him, hand to hand,
I was the champion called to that proud field—
The hope of Greece—nor did I fly nor yield.
Lo ! Troy pours forth again the storm of war,
And sword and spear and torch commingled glare
From her thick ranks—the angry gods are there,
Guiding the fiery tempest to the fleet.
Who now stands forth the battle's rage to meet ?
Where is Ulysses, warrior of the tongue ?
Ye know, O Greeks, that to the foe I sprung,
That this breast was the shield, this arm the stay
Of all your ships, and all your hopes, that day—
For ships and hopes, then saved, now let these arms
      repay.

The arms themselves, arms of the great and brave,

Would, could they speak, me for their master crave.

I plead for them, as loudly they for me,

And Greece will honor both and hear our plea.

Their ancient post of glory to sustain,

Ajax must bear them to the battle plain,

Then shall they shine where charging squadrons
          close,

The pride of Greece, the terror of her foes.

And will Ulysses, in his folly, dare,

With deeds like mine, his exploits to compare?

His Rhesus and his Dolon, slain by night,

His captives and his spoils, all ta'en by sleight,

Naught done by day, nor e'en without the aid

Of Diomede.   If such a price be paid

For such vile deeds, give Diomede his share,

And what is left for Ithacus to wear?

And for what purpose should he strive to gain

Arms he will never use ; for arms are vain

To him who steals upon a sleeping foe :
Who only fights the unarmed, unarmed may go.
The beamy splendor of this helmet see,
And say, thou dastard ! is it fit for thee?
For thee, whom none, but in the dark, e'er dread—
A shining helmet for an ambushed head !
And think'st thou that a neck like thine could e'er
The helmet of Achilles learn to bear?
See, too, the spear his mighty hand has hurled,
And the vast shield, where shines the pictured
        world,
And say, if arms like these may not demand
Far other arm than thine, and other hand ?
Thine, which, to suit thy soul, were only made
To carry on some vile and furtive trade.
Rash fool ! let Greece on thee these arms bestow,
Array thyself, and face the opposing foe—
Dare but one onset on the hostile plain—
Ne'er shall we see, or them, or thee, again ;

For what thou could'st not wield in manly fight,

Would stay the wonted swiftness of thy flight;

A rich and easy prize thou would'st appear,

And all would strive to seize what none would fear.

And why should'st thou another's arms require?

Thine own, untouched by foes, are yet entire :

Thy well kept shield no scar of honor bears—

Mine, shows the fierce thrusts of a thousand spears.

But why this war of words? let deeds declare

The worthiest to wield these arms in war;

Let them amid the opposing host be thrown,

And he who wins them, wear them as his own."

On Visiting the Pennsylvania Hospital.

Whose fair abode is this? whose happy lot
Has drawn them in these peaceful shades to rest,
And hear the distant hum of busy life?
The city's noise, its clouds of smoke and dust,
Vainly invade these leafy walls that wave
On high around it, sheltering all within,
And wooing the scared bird to stay its flight
And add its note of joy to bless the scene:
The city's toils, and cares, and strifes are, sure,
Alike excluded here—Content here smiles
And reigns, and leads her vot'ries through the
     maze
Of flower-embroidered walks to bowers of bliss:

O! 't is a sight to warm the heart of him
Who feels for man, and shares the joys he sees.

My feet have pierced these shades, and I have seen,
Within what seemed so fair, this mansion's tenants :
O ! 't is a sight to chill, to freeze the heart
Of him who feels for man, who pitying views
The wreck of human bliss, and sighs to see
That he can only pity griefs past cure,
And sorrows that no sympathy can soothe.
Here Pleasure never comes, Hope never smiles
But to delude to a more deep despair ;
Here are shut out all joys that sweeten life,
Here are shut in, life's outcasts ; Madness here,
Monarch of terrors, holds his awful court ;
On high-piled human skulls his throne is fixed,
His bursting brows a burning iron crown
Confines, and blends its fires with fiercer flames
That from his ghastly eye-balls wildly glare ;

A robe of straw his giant form conceals;
His hand a leaden sceptre wields, each point
With terrors armed. Ice, never melting, gleams
From the one; from the other, fire unquenchable:
Each, as it points to his devoted prey,
With cold, or heat, or freezes or inflames
The chambers of the brain, and stupefies
And chills to dullest idiocy, or fires
To frenzy's wild unutterable rage.
Such are the throng that here around him wait,
Showing, in all their sad variety,
The awful visitations of his power;
Here the cold gaze of fixed fatuity
Tells that no feeble ray of thought e'er gleams
O'er the wide waste of desolated mind;
Here the wild raving and the maniac yell
Reveal a phantom seated on the throne
Wrested from reason, ruling all within,
Exulting in the never ceasing storm.

I had not sought this scene—my thoughtless steps
Had brought me, where, I knew not, till the sights
And sounds of woe revealed its awful terrors ;
The sudden shock o'ercame me and awakened
A host of these wild fearful images ;
A moment's struggle, and my mind gave way,
And my soul sickened at the awful thought
That I was mad.   I groped in vain to find
Some ray of reason that might light up thought
And consciousness, but all was dark as night :
The horrors of that darkness none can tell ;
Could I recall them all, an age would not
Suffice to tell, what seemed for ages borne.
Man's frail abode in this sad world of change
Is often sung, and heard but as a song :
Death's touch oft wakes his victim to its truth.
As frail as life is reason : both depend
On him who gave them, who can take away
From both, or either, his sustaining arm :

Fear then, thou thankless boaster ! fear the stroke
That throws thy body to the worms, and calls
Thy soul to answer for abused mercies—
Yet fear, still more, the still more fearful doom
That takes the richest of heaven's slighted gifts,
And leaves thy body and thy soul in darkness
To roam the earth a senseless corpse, or gives thee,
Before thy time, to the tormenting fiends.
Such was my crime—with life, health, reason blest,
And heart with rapture glowing, I looked round
On this fair seeming world, and chose its joys
For my sole portion ; scorning all beyond it
As vain and visionary, no warm thought
Of love to him who made me what I was,
E'er kindled its pure flame within my breast,
That burned with earthly and unholy fires ;
I thought not of him, but in doubt or fear ;
I spoke not of him but in jest or wrath.
Such was my punishment ; the beam from heaven,

6*

That pours its light into the mind of man,
Was suddenly extinguished, and a shroud,
Darker than that of death, enveloped all
Within me and around me. In this gloom,
Peopled with spectres, filled with scenes terrific,
How long I lived—if the dread agony
Could life be called—I know not. To the dead
And the condemned, Time measures not his steps,
And every moment seems eternity.

The last verse of John Anderson my jo.

" John Anderson, my jo, John, we clamb the
     hill thegither,
And mony a canty day, John, we've had wi' ane
     anither ;
Now we maun totter down, John, but hand in hand
     we'll go,
And sleep thegither at the foot, John Anderson,
     my jo."

THERE OUGHT TO BE ANOTHER :

John Anderson, my jo, John, from that sleep
     again we'll wake,
When anither day's fair light on our opened eyes
     shall break,

And we'll rise in youth and beauty to that bright
    land to go,
Where life and love shall last for aye, John Ander-
    son, my jo.

OR:

John Anderson, my jo, John, one day we'll waken
    there,
Where a brighter morn than ever shone our opened
    eyes shall cheer,
And in fresh youth and beauty to that blest land
    we'll go,
Where we'll live and love forever, John Anderson,
    my jo.

PIPE CREEK, October 13th, 1842.

A Riddle.

I MADE myself. and though no form have I,
Am fairer than the fairest you can spy;
The sun I outshine in his mid-day light,
And yet am darker than the darkest night;
Hotter I am than fire, than ice more cold,
Richer than purest gems or finest gold,
Yet I am never either bought or sold ;
The man that wants me, never yet was seen;
The poor alone possess me ; yet the mean
And grudging rich oft give me to the poor,
Who yet are not made richer than before ;
The blindest see me, and the deafest hear,
Cowards defy me, and the bravest fear :

If you're a fool, you know me; if you grow
In knowledge, me you will soon cease to know.

Now catch me if you can—I'm sometimes caught,
Though never thought worth catching, never sought.
Am I still hid? then let whoever tries
To see me, give it up, and shut his eyes.

Get me—and low and poor thy state will be;
Forget me—and no equal shalt thou see.

Another Riddle,

MADE FOR OUR AMUSEMENT ONE EVENING.

THERE was a little maiden,
　　And cross and proud was she,
And I loved her very much,
　　And she loved me !

She determined to live single,
　　And I begged and prayed her not,
So at last she married me,
　　And I pitied her hard lot.,

There was another maiden
　　Who hated me, and I
Hated her—she loved her lover
　　Always best when I was by.

When he told his love, to have
    Me present he took care;
And she always answered kindly
    If I was there to hear.

O! many a soft and tender thing
    Was said by lip and eye,
That never had been thought of
    If I had not been nigh.

And now, ye lovely maidens,
    With my presence and advice
You may always turn your lovers
    Into husbands in a trice.

When these love tales you hear, and wish
    To make a kind reply—
Tell all to me, and when you meet
    Take care that I am by.

Now I must tell you who I am,
  Lest some mistake there be :
I am the one that those soft scenes
  You wish should always see.

ζ

Lines,

WRITTEN IN MISS SARAH GAYLE'S ALBUM.

THINE hand, dear little maiden! let me see:
How run the mystic lines of destiny?
The face, too, I must look upon, for there
I used to read more plainly of the fair.
With face and hand, those tell-tales of the heart,
If I have not forgotten all my art,
I may some secrets of thy fate impart.

Now my divining's done—list to the lay
That tells the fortune of thy future day.

Sarah Gayle! thou wilt be fair,
So a thousand youths shall swear ;

And beloved thou shalt be,
And be-rhymed incessantly;
Light the task for lover pale
To sing of lovely Sarah Gayle:
Never will his numbers fail
To tell the charms of Sarah Gayle.
See, they come o'er hill and dale
To gaze in love on Sarah Gayle,
And teach each Alabamian vale
To echo to the name of Gayle.
From distant lands they'll spread the sail,
Hoping to catch a favoring Gayle;
In summer's heat they'll wish a Gayle,
And e'en in winter's storm and hail
They'll still desire to have a Gayle.
If thou should'st frown, they'll sadly wail
With broken hearts for Sarah Gayle;
And many a heavy cotton bale
They'll count light price for smile of Gayle.

Sarah·Gayle! thou wilt be kind,
And perhaps one day inclined
To take a name more to thy mind
Than one that is so much be-rhymed.

Sarah Gayle! be wise as fair ;
E'er thou make that change, beware,
And when thou giv'st away thy name,
Give thy heart also to the claim
Of one who comes with heart as pure
As that he seeks, and name as sure
Unstained and honored to endure.
Sarah Gayle! be good as fair :
Look to heaven—thy home is there;
May this be proph'cy—'t is my prayer.

To my Cousin Mary,

FOR MENDING MY TOBACCO POUCH.

My conscience has given me several twitches
For not having thanked my fair coz. for her stitches;
The pouch that contains the best part of my riches
She has made safe and sound by her excellent stitches;
And whenever I take it from waistcoat or breeches,
I enjoy my quid and admire the stitches.
She has sent me a note all in rhyme also, which is
Still more to be praised than these praise-worthy
    stitches.
I sometimes have seen " few and far between"
    stitches,
The stitchers of which should be thrown in the
    ditches,

For no one need care where such vile things he
  pitches,
And nothing's more vile than such stitchers and
  stitches;
Such stitchers were taught in a time scarce of
  switches,
Or they ne'er would have stitched such detestable
  stitches;
For this saying, I'm told, a sort of distich is
Among the most eminent teachers of stitches:
That experience proves "few and far between"
  switches
Will always produce "few and far between"
  stitches.
But my sweet cousin's skill so much me bewitches,
I must give her a sonnet in praise of her stitches:

Thy stitches are not "few and far between,"
  As other stitches very often are,

And many things beside, as I have seen,
   In this sad world where good things are so rare;
But they are even, neat, and close enough
   My treasured sweets to hold in purest plight;
To keep tobacco safe, and even snuff,
   And thus at once eyes, nose, and mouth delight.

They're like thy smiles, fair cousin, frequent, bright,
   They're like the rows of pearl those smiles dis-
       play ;
They're like the fingers that did make them, white
   And delicate, but not so long as they.

OR:

They're like thy smiles, fair cousin, frequent, bright,
   And ever bringing pleasure in their train ;
They're like thy teeth of pearl, and their pure white,
   Like them, shall never know tobacco's stain.

Then let me view my stores, and all the while
Look on thy stitches, thinking on thy smile—
But ah ! those smiles in distance far are hid,
But here the stitches are—and I will take a quid.

To Mary.

Frown on, ye dark and angry clouds;
   And, Winter, blow that blast again,
That calls thy wrathful host to pour
   Their fury on the wasted plain.

'Tis thus I choose my way to win
   To her whose love my bosom warms;
And brighter seems the prize I seek
   Seen through the gloom of clouds and storms.

Let colder lovers shrink from these,
   And calmly wait for peaceful skies;
Be mine, through toil and pain to win
   The beam of Mary's gladdened eyes.

Perhaps she'll value more my love,
   Perhaps give more of her's to me,
Perhaps may greet me with a smile
   More sweet, if smile more sweet can be.

O! Mary, could'st thou know this heart,
   Could words or deeds its truth declare,
'T would higher raise love's flame in thine,
   Or light it, if it be not there.

To Delia.

Let others heap on heaps their useless ore,
And view with sparkling eyes th' increasing store;
Let others toil, with ceaseless care, to gain
The rich productions of the boundless plain,
And own, each night passed sleepless by their fears,
That wealth has for its joys a thousand cares;
For Fortune's fickle smiles let others pine;
Delia, thy smile, thy witching smile, be mine.
Content, though poor, each easy idle day,
Cheered by that smile, steals unperceived away.
With thy fond arm in mine, when Spring's soft
power
First bursts the bud of every blushing flower,

Then let me guide thy light steps o'er the green,

And show thee all the beauties of the scene;

Or when the sultry suns of Summer pour

A warmer ray, then many a rapturous hour

Awaits us, where the beech-tree's arching shade

Has formed a secret bower for lovers made :

That beech, whose tender rind didst first impart

To Delia the soft secret of my heart—

Carved on whose trunk the faithful vows appear

Which Delia heard not with disdainful ear;

There, by the riv'let's side, we'll careless lay,

And think how transient is a lover's day;

There, will thy swain with fondest zeal prepare

A flowery garland for thy tangled hair;

And thou, with playful hand, a wreath shall join,

And round thy poet's brow thy gift entwine.

With Autumn's ripened fruit when every tree

And shrub hangs loaded, Delia, then for thee

Up to each tall tree's topmost bough I'll spring,

And the full basket to our cottage bring.

To Cowper.

Cowper! who loves not thee deserves not love
From God or man, or aught that God hath formed.
Eloquent pleader for the works of God!
Pleading for all that breathes—from the poor worm
"That crawls at evening in the public path,"
To man, that treads the earth, and looks to heaven.
To the mute wonders of the Almighty hand,
As seen in mountain, valley, field, and flood,
Thou, too, hast given a voice of praise and love;
They speak to all unutterable things,
Till the full heart o'erflows, and pours "the tears
Of holy joy" into the glistening eye
Of him to whom they say—"We all are thine—
Works of a Father's hand, for thee, a child—

8

And given thee but as earnest of the gifts,
Richer than all thy thoughts, that now await
Thy joyful coming to a Father's home.

" O ! worship then with us, while here below,
In this, the vestibule of heaven's high fane,
Whose outer lamps gild the blue vault above thee,
Whose inner courts shall call forth all thy praise."

On Reading Fawcett's Lines

So sings the world's fond slave! so flies the dream
   Of life's gay morn; so sinks the meteor ray
Of fancy into darkness; and no beam
   Of purer light shines on the wanderer's way.

So sings not he who soars on other wings
   Than fancy lends him; whom a cheering faith
Warms and sustains, and whose freed spirit springs
   To joys that bloom beyond the reach of death.

And thou would'st live again! again dream o'er
   The wild and feverish visions of thy youth
Again to wake in sorrow, and deplore
   Thy wanderings from the peaceful paths of truth!

Yet yield not to despair ! be born again,
   And thou shalt live a life of joy and peace,
Shall die a death of triumph, and thy strain
   Be changed to notes of rapture ne'er to cease.

To Mrs. Eleanor Potts,

FOR MANY YEARS AFFLICTED WITH BLINDNESS, ON HEARING
HER PLAY ON THE GUITAR.

I SAT beside an aged saint;
   It was a pleasure there to be,
Her kind and gentle words to hear,
   The calm contented face to see.

She sat in darkness—day's fair light
   Had often come and gone,
Gilding the scenes she long had loved:
   No more for her they shone.

And fond, familiar voices paid
   Affection's homage there;
And as their words of love and truth
   Fell on her charmed ear,

8*

She could but think how great the bliss
  If she again could ever trace
The looks of love she knew were there
  Upon each well-remembered face.

But she had long since felt and said
  Of all this—" It is well;"
And the bowed spirit rose, sustained,
  Its peace and hope to tell.

She sat in darkness ; but the gloom
  Was only in the body's eye,
And covered with the clouds of night
  Only the objects that were nigh.

But the mind's eye that cloud could pierce,
  And things far off descry,
Beyond the bounds of this dull earth
  And its encircling sky.

She sat in darkness; but a light
  Was hers of heavenly ray,
Shining upon a home on high,
  And lighting all her way.

The "light of other days" was hers,
  Of happy days now past and gone;
It called up friends long loved and mourned,
  And sweetly round her shone.

'Twas then, as by her side I sat,
  She softly touched the light guitar,
And tones, that had my childhood charmed,
  Fell, in sweet sadness, on my ear.

I had not heard them since; the sounds
  Thrilled through my quiv'ring frame,
And scenes, and friends, and joys long past,
  Quick at their bidding came.

Those sounds called up a mother's form,
    Her voice, her love, and care,
When at her feet, a happy child,
    I drank with greedy ear

The songs she loved, of power to charm
    And to exalt the heart,
That thoughts and feelings like her own
    They might to me impart.

And if the magic power of song
    Its influence o'er me ever threw,
And haply some small meed of fame
    To lay of mine be ever due,

These early teachings at her knee,
    To these, the high-prized boon I owe,
With all the blessings I have known,
    And all I ever hope to know.

I could but thank her for the strain
  That called up these forgotten lays,
And kindly bade me share with her
  " The light of other days."

And I prayed that the light of the days to come
  Might brighter and brighter prove,
And the gloom of this darkened world be lost
  In the light of the world above.

PIPE CREEK,
October 22d, 1840.

Hymn

FOR THE FOURTH OF JULY, 1832.

BEFORE the Lord we bow—
The God who reigns above,
And rules the world below,
Boundless in power and love.
Our thanks we bring,
In joy and praise,
Our hearts we raise
To heaven's high King.

The nation thou hast blest
May well thy love declare,
Enjoying peace and rest,
Protected by thy care.

For this fair land,
  For this bright day,
  Our thanks we pay—
Gifts of thine hand !

Our fathers sought thee, Lord !
  And on thy help relied ;
Thou heard'st and gav'st the **word,**
  And all their need supplied.
    Led by thy hand
      To victory,
      They hailed a free
    And rescued land.

God of our sires ! that hand
  Be now, as then, displayed
To give this favored land
  Thy never-failing aid.

Still may it be
Thy fixed abode!
Be thou our God!
Thy people we!

May every mountain height,
Each vale and forest green,
Shine in thy word's pure light,
And its rich fruits be seen!
May every tongue
Be tuned to praise,
And join to raise
A grateful song!

Earth! hear thy Maker's voice,
The great Redeemer own;
Believe, obey, rejoice :
Bright is the promised crown.

Cast down thy pride,
   Thy sin deplore,
   And bow before
The crucified.

And when in power he comes,
   O, may our native land,
From all its rending tombs,
   Send forth a glorious band!
     A countless throng
       Ever to sing,
       To heaven's high King,
     Salvation's song!

9

A Bear Story.

THERE was a Bear—alas! that we must bear
The loss of such a bear.   He was the pet
And plaything of the children, men, and maids;
The ladies, too, wept briny tears for him,
'Till all the springs were salt.   For much he loved
To play his tricks before them, and to take
From their fair hands the dainties they would bring;
And they would stroke his sable fur, and feel
His velvet paws; and then he licked his paws,
And paws so touched, he could have licked, and
        lived
Long on such licking.   But, alas! he died.—
Now a bare bear-skin, and some bare bear bones.

Are all that's left of Bruin—save at night
When blaze the lights upon the mountain side,
And music o'er the valley floats, and calls
The bright-eyed maidens to the sprightly dance—
Upon the glossy curls that shade the cheek
And brow of beauty, Bruin's fat is there,
Soft'ning and polishing the silken locks.
Bruin, thy chops were savory—so said
The chaps that did thereon their chops regale ;
The ladies ate thee not—they would not feed
Upon a tame and educated bear ;
Nor me, could steak or cutlet, fried or broiled,
Stewed paw, or garnished head, tempt to that feast;
For I had seen thy death.   It was a death
Unseemly for a bear, unworthy of thy race.
But had'st thou died among thy native wilds,
When hound, and horse, and horn, had from thy lair
Aroused thee, and thou nobly stood'st at bay,
And many a fierce foe howled his last, within

Thy perilous embrace, and gallant hunters
Closed round thee slowly, marking thy dread glance,
Admiring thy stern courage, giving death
In honorable wounds;—then had'st thou died
A death of glory, and had I been one
Of that proud ring, I could have joined the feast
Won by fair chase, and combat—eat thy steaks
And picked thy bones unscrupulous.   Alas!
Far other was thine end; a felon's death
The cowards gave thee; threw around thy neck
A noose, and thrice essayed to drag thee back
As a vile prisoner.

    Once when escaped, I marked
His noble bearing, when his fierce pursuers
Fled from his glance.   He looked upon the mount-
  ain.
And I then hoped to see him climb its top
And turn, and growl defiance.   One there was
Of courage dauntless in the crowd of foes.

Cæsar. by name, Cæsar by nature too.
He calls to Bruin as he slow retires,
In words of scorn and menace.   Quick he turns—
They meet—they close—more doubtful conflict
      never
Did battle-field display.   Well were they matched :
Both brave, both black, and equal both in height,
For Bruin boldly raised himself erect
Upon his hinder limbs, and brandished high
And huge as giant's arms, his fierce fore-paws.
Soon Cæsar, seized with dext'rous jerk, the rope
Pendant from Bruin's neck—as soon, the paws
Of Bruin, o'er the shoulders broad, and back
Of Cæsar, closed in deadly grip : that hug
There was no standing, and so Cæsar tripped him—
For Bruin, though he stood on two feet well,
Had never practiced one in his gymnastics :
He falls, Cæsar above him ; still the strife
Is desperate.   And lo ! now Bruin turns

9*

Upon him with a growl, and fiercer grasp.
Now, Cæsar! ply thy rope—thy life depends
Upon the hold it takes ; thy foe's strong throat
Must be compressed that not a breath may pass.
Thy ribs now almost touch, the heart scarce beats
Between them, quivers, and must soon be still.
One other little breath, one other strain
Of those strong arms—and Cæsar is no more.
That other breath comes not ; one desperate pull,
And the rope closed the passage.   See—he gasps ;
One last convulsive struggle ends the strife.
Those mighty paws, now weak as baby's hands,
Cæsar has thrown aside.   His heart has room
Again to beat—he rises conqueror.
Such was the end of Bruin.   Yet before
That fierce encounter, other means were tried
To lure him back to bondage.   It was said
" Music had charms to soothe the savage breast,"
And that he often seemed, when the full tones

Of richest harmony flowed from the lips
Of his kind mistress, to drink in the sounds
With rapture, like all other listeners.
Music was therefore tried. The band was called,
And captivating were the strains they poured
In Bruin's ears ; but it was vain, for he
Would not be captivated. Then they called
Two of that band, with voices sweet as notes
Of nightingale, of power to charm the ear
Of every listener, and calm the heart
With all the magic influence of song.
They came and breathed in sweetest melody
A plaintive ditty to this angry bear,
Beseeching him to lay aside his wrath,
Resume his chain, and live among his friends.
He heard, and heeded not. And when you hear
The song that he received so sullenly,
You'll wonder that the bear was such a brute,
And think he justly died. The song ran thus

SONG.

O. BRUIN! O, Bruin! come back to thy chain,
Nor seek thy far home o'er the mountain again,
For the mother that bore thee will know thee no
    more,
And thy brother cubs drive thee away from the
    door.

Why would'st thou return where thou nightly must
    howl
In thy hunger, as through the dark forest you
    prowl
To fight the wild bees for their hoard of sweet food,
Or spoil thy teeth cracking the nuts of the wood?
What a life thou hast led since thou haply wast
    caught,
And here to this sweet little valley wast brought!

Its blest waters thy drink, its rich dainties thy fare :
What more could be wished for man, woman, or bear ?

It is true you are tied ; but, Bruin, you know
It is all for your good that you are kept so ;
How many are here who would gladly agree
To be tied to a tree, could they fatten like thee.

We have tamed you, and fed you, and now, you are
        here,
Your polite education engages our care ;
Your manners are mended, some clever things
        taught,
But greater attainments are still to be sought.

Carusi is here, and shall teach you to dance,
How to enter the ball-room, and bow, and advance
To the ladies, who sit in a beautiful row,
Each waiting to see if the bear 'll be her beau.

Then. the waltzing—O, Bruin! think only of that.
Of a lady's bare arms with thy bear arms enwrapt ;
Thy bear-skin, her bare skin shall touch ; O ! what
　　　bear
Can bear any pleasure with this to compare ?

And think of thy paws—when the dancing is done,
And the summer is o'er, and the ladies are gone,
Through the long winter nights, when the snow
　　　flakes fall thick,
Thy lady-pressed paws will be luscious to lick.

August 25th, 1838.

Creation.

" Tous ces vastes pays d'azure et de lumière
   Tirés du sein du vide, formés sans matière,
   Arrondis sans compas, et tournants sans pivot,
   Ont à peine coutés la depense d'un mot."
                                  VOLTAIRE.

" By night the atheist half believes a God."

FROM the dark depth of nature's void arise
Unnumbered worlds, and glitter in the skies.
No bright materials the vast orbs demand,
Nor rule, nor compass, nor a forming hand;
Self-poised their axes, self-sustained their poles,
A universe of wonders o'er us rolls.
They were not, and were called; were called and
      heard,
And cost, and scarcely cost, the effort of a word.

Written for the Coronation

OF THE TWELFTH-NIGHT QUEEN.

HERE is a crown, but where is the Queen
With brow of beauty, and grace of mien,
  And worthy such gift to demand?
Whose power all hearts shall ever confess,
Whose smile shall bless and frown depress,
  And every look command?

Such is the Queen to whom we bow;
Thine, fair Catherine, is the brow
  To adorn the crown we bring,
And she shall reign our chosen Queen,
With her brow of beauty and grace of mien,
  Till she chooses to take a king.

Here's crown and Queen, but where shall she reign?
What loyal subjects and fair domain
     Shall we to our Queen impart?
Her empire shall be
O'er the land and the sea,
     And her throne in every heart.

10

Translation from Martial.

To-morrow he will live, Lorenzo swears,
Quite a new life; and hath so sworn for years.
Tell me, Lorenzo, when will come this day
Thou call'st to-morrow? Is it still distant? Say.
Where is it, and how is 't to be got?
What is the price at which it may be bought?'
Will it by Parry at the pole be found?
Or brought to light by Semnes from under ground?
To-morrow, did'st thou say, Lorenzo? Why,
Is that a day that hath not yet gone by?
 Twas known before the flood; its years outweigh
E'en those of Nestor, or Methusaleh.
To-morrow thou wilt live! To-day is quite
Too late; he who lived yesterday, did right.

To a Rose-bud.

Ah ! why so tardy, timid Rose,
 Thy opening beauties to display ?
Ah ! why within their mossy cell
 So long thy shrinking petals stay ?

Full many a morn, and many an eve,
 Thy gently swelling bud I've seen.
And fondly strove, with many a kiss,
 To wake thee from thy bed of green.

When, scarcely formed, you first appeared,
 I marked thee with a lover's eye,
And doomed thee to an envied fate—
 On Delia's breast to live and die.

Spring's golden smile now gilds the plain,
  And chases Winter's frown away:
To thee, O Rose! she fondly calls,
  And pours on thee her warmest ray.

Already doth her golden smile
  My Delia's glowing beauties grace:
Already hath her pencil bright
  Tinged with its radiant hue her face.

With that same hue, O happy Rose,
  She longs thy velvet leaves to tip,
And breathe on them the same perfume
  She breathed on Delia's dewy lip.

Near thee the lately wakened bees,
  Anxious to taste thy beauties, stay;
With me thy promised bloom they wait,
  And wonder at thy long delay.

Then haste, and when, with anxious step,
    Thy growth to mark, I next shall walk,
Then let me see thy blushing head
    Bend with its dewy weight thy stalk.

10*

To a Golden Key.

LONG had a golden key concealed
   The treasures of my Delia's breast;
Treasures one half so sweet and rich
   Sure never key before possessed.

The ponderous key that guards his wealth,
   If the rich miser would bestow,
Gladly the proffered boon I'd seize,
   'Tis almost all I wish below.

But ah! that litle golden key,
   Could I but dare unlock its store,
And with the trembling hand of Love
   Those treasures, long concealed, explore.

In vain would then the miser's wealth,
    In vain the wealth of worlds would bribe me
To break the silken ties with which
    The little urchin Love has tied me.

Delia! too long upon that heaven
    Hath slept th unconscious key of gold,
Enjoyed a bliss it cannot feel—
    For. trust me, Delia. it is cold.

Then take another, who would prize
    That heaven as a monarch s throne,
A key who. by thy goodness chained,
    Forever will his bondage own.

O ! let me be the happy key
    To guard the treasures of thy heart,
And from its fondly treasured trust
    That key shall never, never part.

Stanzas.

FAREWELL, ye once delightful scenes ! farewell!
  No more your charms can soothe my aching
    heart :
These long-drawn sighs. these flowing tears, can
    tell
  How much I grieve, sweet scenes ! from you to
    part.

For once these glassy streams, these smiling plains,
  The little sorrows of my soul could ease,
But now each long-known spot augments my
    pains,
  From sad remembrance how it once could please.

Oft in the glistening dews that gemmed you mead,
  Blithesome I've bathed my tiny, truant feet,
When some wild gambol lured my jocund tread,
  To seek from tyrant eyes some lone retreat.

Here sported I, when, on swift pinions borne,
  The airy minutes of my childhood flew ;
And here arose my youth's effulgent morn,
  And not a threatening cloud appeared in view.

But soon, ah soon ! misfortune's blackest gloom
  The radiance of the opening dawn o'ercast,
Nor left one ray of comfort to illume
  The horrors of the melancholy waste.

Here first—incautious fool to bless the day—
  I saw my Delia bounding o'er the plains :
I saw, and gave my soul a willing prey
  To Love's soft bondage. and embraced my chains.

118   KEY'S POEMS.

On her the potent queen of love bestowed
   Her own sweet smile, her own soul-stealing grace ;
Her warm heart with its soft emotion glowed,
   And shone in every feature of her face.

A vivid rose-bud opening to the view
   Then did she shine, in life's and beauty's morn.
With the rash hand of eager youth I flew,
   Snatched at the flower, regardless of the thorn.

But ah ! too late I felt the bitter smart,
   Too deep I feel it in each throbbing vein ;
Far hence, alas !   I bear a bleeding heart,
   Nor hope to find a solace for my pain.

For nature cursed me not with soul so cool
   That time or absence can its griefs remove ;
No—reason's cold and unimpassioned rule
   Sways not a bosom fired with luckless love.

No, Delia! by those soft and tender sighs
 Which pity drew from that soft breast of thine,
By that fair hand which wiped my streaming eyes,
 And by those eyes which mixed their tears with
  mine—

By these I swear thy image from my breast
 No time, no absence, ever shall remove;
Where'er I rove, with thy remembrance blest,
 I 'll doat upon the agonies of love.

To my Steed.

'Tis sweet to breathe freely the balmy air,
    And walk where we will, at morn, eve, or noon,
When the step keeps time with the bounding heart,
    And the strings of life are all in tune.

'Tis sweet to be rocked on the ocean's swell
    When the fresh breeze fills the sail,
And the light bark leaps o'er the dancing waves,
    And laughs at the rising gale.

But give me the steady and fearless seat
    On the back of the gallant steed
That knows no check to his flying feet
    But the hand that rules his speed!

Written at the White Sulphur Springs.

A word of advice about matters and things
May be useful to people who come to these springs :
First, there's a bell in the morning that rings
To awaken the people who come to the springs,
And the folks fix their ribbons and tie up their
      strings,
And look very beautiful here at the springs.

There's an insect or two, called a flea, that here
      stings
The skins of the people who stay at the springs ;
There's a broom and a half here, for nobody brings
Such implements here. to sweep out the springs :

11

There's a maid and a half, too, for one of them
swings
Rather much to one side; for she's lame at the
springs.

There's a bawling all day—but the ball at night
clings
The most to my fancy of all at the springs—
To conclude, though some things here might do e'en
for kings,
If you wish to fare well, say farewell to the springs.

Petition for a Habeas Corpus.

To the Honorable James Sewall Morsell, one
Of the Judges of the county of Washington:

May it please your honor to hear the petition
Of a poor old mare in a miserable condition,
Who has come this cold night to beg that your honor
Will consider her case and take pity upon her.
Her master has turned her out in the street,
And the stones are too hard to lie down on, or eat;
Entertainment for horses she sees every where,
But, alas! there is none, as it seems, for a mare.
She has wandered about, cold, hungry, and weary,
And can't even get in the Penitentiary,

For the watchmen all swear it is more than they
  dare,
Or Mr. Edes either, to put the mayor there.
So she went to a lawyer to know what to do.
And was told she must come and lay her case be-
  fore you,
That you an injunction or ha. cor. would grant :
And if that means hay and corn. it is just what I
  want.
Your petitioner, therefore, prays that your honor
  will not fail,
To send her to a stable and her master to jail ;
And such other relief to grant as your honor may
  think meet,
Such as chopped straw or oats, for an old mare to eat.
With a trough full of these and a rack full of hay,
Your petitioner will ever, as in duty bound, pray.

Philip Barton Key,

IF nature's richest gifts could ever,
If genius, wit, and eloquence, could charm,
If grief of sorrowing friends, or anguish wild
That wrings the widow's and the orphan's heart,
Could sooth stern death, and stay th' uplifted stroke,
Long had this victim of his wrath been spared.

Mourning survivors! let all care give place
To that great care that most demands your thoughts :
The care that brings the troubled soul to Christ ;
Fix there your hopes.   There is, beyond the grave,
A life of bliss. where death shall never more
Part you from joys that know no bound nor end.

11*

William Hemsly, Esq.,

WHO DIED IN 1826.

HERE lies a man whose life proved and adorned
The faith by which he walked.   By all esteemed,
By many loved, hated or feared by none,
He moved, secluded from the world's vain gaze,
Within a narrow, but a glorious sphere
Of Christian duty, shedding love and peace
Around his path, where many an eye that once
Beheld and blessed him, now is dim with tears.
Reader! if thou dost know the grace of God,
Thank Him for this His gift; and pray that thou
May'st live, like Hemsly, to thy Maker's praise,
And, like him, die with steadfast hope in Christ,
The victor, not the victim, of the grave!

Isabella M. Steele,

WHY must the grave hide one whose light would
    shine
To bless the world? Why friends and kindred
    mourn?
And this cold stone—why must it vainly strive
To tell a mother's love, a mother's grief?

The grave must hide the young, the fair, the good,
To prove the grave to be the gate of life
Through which they pass to joys that bloom not
    here.
Kindred and friends must mourn, that they may
    long

To meet again, where they shall part no more.

A mother's heart must bleed that He who wounds

Only to heal, may call its hopes from earth

To fix them with a sainted child in heaven.

When graves give up their dead, O! then may all

Who weep o'er this, reap blessings from their tears.

Sarah M. Steele,

WHO DEPARTED THIS LIFE APRIL 10TH, 1828,
IN THE 23D YEAR OF HER AGE.

ALL that the world can promise to the hope
Of the young heart was hers, and in her heart
Dwelt every gentle and endearing virtue
That gives to life its bliss.   The summons came
To call her from her mother s arms, to lie
By a loved sister's grave, whose peaceful death
Shone as a light to guide her through the gloom
Of the dark path she was so soon to tread.

And shall we mourn o er relics such as these?
And fear this earth will not give up her dead?
Hath He not risen victor of the grave?
Shone not this hope upon her parting hour?
  Lord! we believe: help thou our unbelief."

Mrs. Mary Ann Worsell,

WHO DEPARTED THIS LIFE, APRIL, 1831,
IN THE 32D YEAR OF HER AGE.

"A LITTLE while," this narrow house, prepared
By grief and love, shall hold the blessed dead ;
"A little while," and she who sleeps below
Shall hear the call to rise and live forever;
"A little while," and ye who pour your tears
On this cold grave, shall waken in your own,
And ye shall see her, in her robes of light,
And hear her song of triumph.   Would ye then
Partake with her the bliss of that new life ?
Tread now the path she brightly marked before ye !
Choose now her Lord ! live now her life ! and yours
Shall be her hope and victory in death.

George Murdock,

WHO DIED IN 1812.

A LIFE beneficent, mild, useful, just,
Marked him who rests below; the warm good-will
Of all who knew him, and the tear that springs
E'en now at memory's bidding from the heart,
Warmly attest his worth. His, too, at death—
Rich fruit of such a life—was the calm hour
When conscience breathes that whisper to the soul
Which speaks of peace, and prompts the humble hope
Of heaven's benign acceptance. Thus to live,
And thus to die, O, reader! be thy care.

Johannes J. Sayrs.

" Hujus ecclesiæ rector primus hic quo,.
Christi servus, fideliter ministrabat,
Sepultus, jacet."

HERE once stood forth a man who from the world,
Though bright its aspect to the youthful eye,
Turned with affection ardent to his God,
And lived and died an humble minister
Of His benignant purposes to man.
Here lies he now; yet grieve not thou for him,
Reader! He trusted in that love where none
Have ever vainly trusted.   Rather let
His marble speak to thee; and should'st thou feel
The rising of a new and solemn thought.

Waked by this sacred place and sad memorial,
O, listen to its impulse!—'tis divine—
And it shall lead thee to a life of peace,
A death of hope, and endless bliss hereafter.

12

Lines given to William Darlington,

A DEAF AND DUMB BOY.

THE dumb shall speak, and the deaf shall hear,
  In the brighter days to come,
When they've passed through the troubled scenes
      of life
  To a higher and happier home.

They shall hear the trumpet's fearful blast,
  And the crash of the rending tomb,
And the sinner's cry of agony,
  As he wakes to his dreaded doom.

And the conqueror's shout, and the ransomed's song,
  On their opened ears shall fall;
And the tongue of the dumb, in the chorus of praise,
  Shall be louder and higher than all.

O, Thou ! whose still voice can need no ear
   To the heart its message to bear !
Who canst hear. the unuttered reply of the heart,
   As it glows in the fervor of prayer,

Speak in thy pity and power to these
   Who only Thee can hear :
And bend, to the call of their speaking hearts,
   Thine ever-listening ear.

Home.

O ! WHERE can the soul find relief from its foes,
A shelter of safety, a home of repose?
Can earth's brightest summit, or deepest hid vale,
Give a refuge no sorrow nor sin can assail?
          No, no, there's no home !
There's no home on earth ; the soul has no home.

Shall it leave the low earth, and soar to the sky,
And seek an abode in the mansions on high?
In the bright realms of bliss shall a dwelling be given,
And the soul find a home in the glory of heaven?
          Yes, yes, there's a home?
There's a home in high heaven : the soul has a home !

O ! holy and sweet its rest shall be there,
Free forever from sin, from sorrow and care;
And the loud hallelujahs of angels shall rise
To welcome the soul to its home in the skies.
>Home, home, home of the soul!
The bosom of God is the home of the soul.

12*

Translation from Buchanan's

Who has not stood and silent gazed
    Upon the countless orbs of light
Rolling in brightness through the sky
    To gild and beautify the night:

Or seen at morn the burning wheels
    That upward bear th' awakened sun,
Scattering the darkness from the path
    In which his glorious race is run!

Like a decked bridegroom—on his brows
    A dazzling crown of gems and gold—
He comes, and the far eastern waves
    Leap up his glory to behold.

He mounts the heights of heaven. and like
   A giant with a hundred hands,
Flings wide his gifts of light and life,
   Beauty and joy, to distant lands ;

And, when his mighty work is done,
   Seeks his pavilion in the west,
And sinks in robes of radiant gold,
   Mild and majestic, to his rest.

The Nobleman's Son.

"Yesterday, at the seventh hour, the fever left him."—St. John, iv., 52.

THERE'S a lordly hall on Capernaum's heights,
    Magnificent, costly, and fair,
And within and without the gay delights
    Of the rich and the great are there.

But the dwellings of earth, whether high or low,
    Or mighty and massive their walls,
Cannot keep in joy, or keep out woe—
    They must open when misery calls.

And sorrow, and sickness, and death will come
    When sent, and with step as sure
They pass through the gates of the gilded dome
    As the cottager's open door.

That courtly hall its gay light throws
    No more on Capernaum's hill ;
All dark and sad in the gloom of its woes,
    The songs of its gladness still.

In a lonely chamber a fair child lies,
    Of that noble house the loved heir,
The joy and pride of a mother's eyes,
    And a father's fondest care.

And that mother is there, with looks that now
    Of a mother's agony speak ;
And her hand oft presses his throbbing brow,
    And her lips his burning cheek.

And the father is gone, in his fear and his grief,
    The pitying aid to implore
Of Him, who has never refused relief
    To the cry of the wretched and poor.

Through the night, through the day, she has
 watched; to his home
 He returns not : the faint hope is gone
That the mighty One he seeks will come
 To heal her dying son.

To her fond caress there is no return,
 Yet her arms she around him folds,
And the quickening pulses beat and burn
 In the little hand she holds.

Now she holds that hand, and she looks, in her fear,
 In the face of her dying boy,
And there falls in its burning palm a tear—
 She has started with sudden joy,

For on that hand she clasped, so dear,
 A healthful coolness came ;
It seemed as if the mother's tear
 Had quenched the fever's flame.

To the face on which she so tearfully gazed
    The wondrous change extends,
As his head from his pillow he gently raised,
    And his eye on his mother bends.

On his rosy lips she kisses the dew,
    And his forehead calm and fair,
And she sees that the light, in his eyes of blue,
    Of love alone, is there.

It was not the tear, by a mother shed,
    That the pains of that sickness allayed :
"Go thy way, thy son liveth !" the Lord had said,
    Was believed, and the fever obeyed.

O ! ye, in unbelieving fear,
    Who weep o'er those you love,
When sickness, pain, or death appear,
    Your faith and trust to prove :

O ! know ye how and where to seek
    That mighty One, who here
Vouchsafed these words of life to speak,
    And heard this father's prayer?

His heart is still soft pity's throne,
    His ear as open stands,
His hand as strong, and still alone
    His word the world commands.

And He is nigh thee! on thy heart
    That pitying hand is laid,
And every wish thy lips impart
    Is to that ear conveyed.

" Ask what thou wilt," commands He still;
    Fear not, thou shalt be heard;
Only believe—He can, He will
    Speak the life-giving word..

It may not be that life that spends
   In care and pain its breath,
That runs its weary course, and ends
   At last, and soon, in death.

But a gift beyond thy poor request
   May to thy prayers be given :
A life to be spent in the mansions of **rest**,
   And the endless bliss of heaven.

January, 1843.

13

Written for the Bethel Church at Havre.

To thee, O God! whose awful voice
    Earth, sea, and air obey,
This humble house of prayer we raise,
    And here our homage pay.

Its Bethel flag floats in the breeze,
    Its stars on the ocean shine.
And the weary mariner's heart is cheered,
    As he hails the holy sign.

The ship at rest, their perils past,
    The joyous seamen come
Where the Bethel flag its welcome waves—
    The flag of their distant home.

O God! if the heart's warm thanks to thee
A grateful offering prove.
If prayer and praise can rise on wings
Of gratitude and love,

Here in this house high hymns of joy
Thy rescued sons shall raise,
And glowing hearts and ready tongues
Their great Protector praise.

They've seen thy works upon the sea,
Thy wonders in the deep,
When thou didst loose the stormy winds
O'er the raging waves to sweep.

They sunk to the ocean's lowest depths,
They rose on the mountain wave,
They hung on the brink of the dread abyss,
That yawned as an open grave.

They called on thee, and the raging sea
    Sunk down at thy command,
And the angry rush of the winds was hushed
    In the grasp of thy mighty hand.

O ! let them come, and this holy flag
    Shall float in sainted air,
As high they raise the hymn of praise,
    And the heart's ascending prayer.

And the breath of heaven shall fill their sails
    Wherever a breeze shall blow,
And they shall bear the gospel's light
    Wherever a wave shall flow.

And thus, O God ! the boundless sea
    Thy glory shall proclaim,
And its distant isles' lone shores resound
    With the Redeemer's name.

March, 1841.

Sunday School Celebration,

JULY FOURTH, 1833.

SING, all ye nations! the arm of the Lord
Is revealed in its power, fulfilling His word.

Ye watchmen of Zion, the glory beholding,
   Long promised, now dawning to gladden our eyes,
Shout aloud, through all lands the bright vision un-
         folding,
   And call Zion's hosts to awake, and arise!
      Sing, all ye nations, etc.,

Roll on, thou glad Earth, thy dark places are gleam-
         ing
   With light from on high, and the new-risen ray

13*

On thy far distant mountains and lone isles is
    beaming,
    And the nations awaken, and hail the bright day.
        Sing, all ye nations, etc.

Roll on in thy path, till the radiance, increasing,
    Its noon-day effulgence around thee shall fling,
And thy people all join in hosannas unceasing,
    To praise their Creator, Redeemer, and King!
        Sing, all ye nations, etc.

Thou shalt shine in that light, and the beams of thy
    splendor
    The far wilds of the west shall exultingly see;
Thou shalt join in that song, the loudest to render
    Thy rapturous homage, fair land of the free!
        Sing, all ye nations, etc.

Fair land of the free! thou wast made to be ever
    A refuge and home for the poor and oppressed,

And thy welcome and blessing denied shall be never
To the wanderer who flees to thy bosom for rest.
Sing, all ye nations, etc.

Fair land of the free! the lamp thou hast lighted
Still sheds its pure lustre on Liberty's shrine;
And the nations awaken, enlightened, united,
To partake of thy bliss, in thy triumph to join.
Sing, all ye nations, etc.

Fair land of the free! may that light that for ever
Gives freedom and life, pour its brightness on
thee!
Shed around thee the light of salvation, and never
Be darkness in thee, thou fair land of the free.
Sing, all ye nations, etc.

The Lord Will Hear Thee.

"Will the Lord cast off for ever? and will he be favorable no more?

"Is his mercy clean gone for ever? doth his promise fail for evermore?

"Hath God forgotten to be gracious? hath he in anger shut up his tender mercies?

"And I said, This is my infirmity; but I will remember the years of the right hand of the Most High.

"I will remember the works of the Lord: surely I will remember thy wonders of old."—PSALM lxxvii.

WILL God absent himself for evermore,
   Nor hear again my supplicating cry?
Is mercy gone for ever? and the day
   Of his felt presence utterly passed by?

Hath he resolved his wonted grace no more
  Shall wait upon his people s earnest prayer ?
His loving kindness turned to wrath, and man
  But left to pray and perish in despair ?

This cannot be, O thou of little faith ;
  'Tis thine own weakness that suggests thy fears :
The God thou seek'st can know no change, his truth
  Steadfast abides through everlasting years.

And if before his face erect in hope
  Thou can'st not stand, then prostrate fall and
      pray,
And then his hands shall raise thee up, and soon
  The clouds of doubt and fear shall roll away.

Call to remembrance former days, and see
  If faithful heart e er offered fruitless prayer ;
If God, commanding all to seek his face,
  E'er turned from any with unpitying ear.

And look through time to that eternal day
When high shall sound the rapturous hymn of
       praise,
"Thou doest all things well, O Lord! and just
And true, O King of kings, are all thy ways."

Thou in that song shalt join; the darkness past
That from thy view the answering God concealed,
The unheeded blessings of his unseen hand,
And all the wonders of his love revealed.

Then shalt thou see a Father's tender care
Displayed alike in all withheld and given:
Given—to increase thy love, and fix thy trust;
Withheld—to wean from earth and fit for heaven.

Then shalt thou see how every prayer was heard:
The ill thy blindness asked, refused; the good
Delayed, to keep thee waiting on his word;
Thy waiting blest—the blessing then bestowed.

Then fear not ; that petition that so oft
    And warmly thou hast pressed, is not cast out ;
Still wait on God ! still seek, and hope, and trust,
    Till light shall shine through every shade of
        doubt.

Though rich the boon, to which thy heart aspires,
    'Tis not too vast from boundless power to flow ;
Nor canst thou fear to ask what boundless love
    Can never be unwilling to bestow.

Then press thy suit undoubtingly to God,
    Who best knows when to grant—when to refuse ;
And leave the way, and time, and all to him—
    Let not thy folly, but his wisdom, choose.

And rest in this, that whatsoe'er thy prayer
    Humbly and faithfully of God requires,
He will fulfil—or otherwise bestow
    A gift still richer than thy prayer desires.

Would'st thou rejoice t'obtain whate'er thou seek'st?
  Nor more rejoice, if from his boundless store,
Kind, above all that thou canst ask or think,
  Thy Father in his bounty gives thee more.

'Tis true thou art unworthy to be heard,
  But make thy want, and not thy worth, thy plea;
There is One worthy all that thou canst ask,
  Who gives himself, and all his worth, to thee.

Then come, come boldly, to the throne of grace:
  There stands an Advocate thy cause to gain;
Ask in his name—ask what thou wilt—his love
  Assures thee that thou shalt not ask in vain.

What is Death? Is it the End of Life?

Who doubts that there is a God? Who can look around him, without seeing that everything bears witness to him, and to his power, justice, and goodness? He that sees only this, cannot believe that death is the end of life.

Look at the man that throughout his life has known nothing but the uses and abuses of prosperity—who has never thanked God for anything, and hardened his heart against all thoughts of him.

In the midst of his pomp and pleasure, when the music of the world sounds sweetest in his ear, and his heart dances with joy, death comes to him. If God be just, can death be the end of life to him?

Yes, it may be said, the sufferings of death in

14

such a man show the justice of God sufficiently. Death is terrible to him that is at ease in his possessions.   If he looks no further than to the darkness of the grave, does not the torment of feeling that he is cast down from his high place—that he is to be thrust into the earth, and given to its worms —more than out-weigh a life of worldly pleasure? And he will, he must, look further.   Conscience, whose whispers he could drown in the din of the world's madness, now thunders, and he trembles— and who can tell what amount of agony may not be crowded into the last few days, or even hours, of such a life, making that brief space enough for just and tremendous retribution?   This may be allowed—still the worldling sometimes falls, and there is no such space.   The stroke comes suddenly, and he is gone in a moment!   Gone where? to annihilation? where God's arm cannot reach him?   No! Death cannot be the end of life to him.

Look at that aged saint! He has passed the
world's trials; he has been acquainted with the
" sweet uses of adversity," and learned wisdom, and
seen God's hand in many blessings, and learned
love. He is at peace. The evening of his days
has come, his work is almost done; the discipline
of this life is passed, the world's cares are laid
aside, and his treasure and his thoughts are in heav-
en. " He knows in whom he has believed," and is
waiting for his summons.

And what is that summons for which all things
in a long life of probation have been preparing him?
for which joys and sorrows, hopes and fears, helps
and hindrances, trials and temptations, have been
teaching, and enlightening, and purifying, and
strengthening him? Is it to perish in a grave?
Impossible—God cannot have made such a work for
such an end.

The man has been taught by everything within

him and around him, and made to feel and know that he is immortal. God's own word has been given him, and he has made it "a lamp to his feet, and a light to his path," and it has never failed him. Is it now to go out in darkness? Will the God who has been proving his truth and justice to him all his days, suffer him to be cheated at the last? Impossible.

Consider his improvement—look at the advances he has made, by his discipline here, in all that ennobles man. God himself has taught him by his Spirit, led him by his hand, armed him for the conflict with sin and temptation, and given him the victory; will he now deny him the crown, and give him to the grave?

Has God purified his heart by faith, elevated him above the world, subdued his passions, healed his infirmities, given him holy and heavenly affections, and made him a fit associate for angels; and will

he now give him to the worms? Impossible—
death cannot be the end of life to him. No—it is
the beginning of life. His death is the death of
the seed cast into the earth, that shooteth up with
renewed vigor rich in the fruits and flowers of an-
other life. His death is the death of the worm
that spinneth her shroud and dieth, to rise again a
joyous and blessed thing, and spread her new wings
in the breath of heaven, telling, wherever she flies,
that God is great and good, and that death is not
the end of life.

January 29th.

14*

The Worm's Death-Song.

O ! LET me alone—I've a work to be done
   That can brook not a moment's delay ;
While yet I breathe I must spin and weave,
   And may rest not night nor day.

Food and sleep I will never know
   Till my blessed work be done ;
Then my rest shall be sweet, in the winding-sheet
   That around me I have spun.

I have been a base and grovelling thing,
   And the dust of the earth my home,
But now I know that the end of my woe,
   And the day of my bliss, is come.

In the shroud I make, this creeping frame
   Shall peacefully die away,
But its death shall be new life to me,
   In the midst of its perished clay.

I shall wake, I shall wake, a glorious form
   Of brightness and beauty to wear;
I shall burst from the gloom of my opening tomb,
   And breathe in the balmy air.

I shall spread my new wings to the morning sun,
   On the summer's breath I'll live;
I will bathe me where, in the dewy air,
   The flowers their sweetness give.

I will not touch the dusty earth,
   I'll spring to the brightening sky,
And, free as the breeze, wherever I please,
   On joyous wing I'll fly.

And wherever I go, timid mortals may know
  That, like me, from the tomb they shall rise;
To the dead shall be given, by signal from heaven,
  A new life, and new home in the skies.

Then let them, like me, make ready their shrouds,
  Nor shrink from the mortal strife,
And like me they shall sing, as to heaven they
    spring,
  Death is not the end of life.

    January 31st, 1841.

"All things are yours."

1 CORINTHIANS iii. 21.

BEHOLD the grant the King of kings
    Hath to his subjects given :
"All things are yours," it saith ; all things
    That are in earth and heaven.

The saints are yours, to guide you home,
    And bless you with their prayers ;
The world is yours, to overcome
    Its pleasures and its cares :

And life is yours, to give it all
    To works of faith and love :
And death is yours, a welcome call
    To higher joys above ;

All present things are yours : whate'er
  God's providence decreed.
Is from his treasures culled with care,
  And sent to suit thy need ;

And things to come are yours ; and all
  Shall ever ordered be,
To keep thee safe, whate'er befall,
  And work for good to thee :

And Christ is yours—his sacrifice,
  To speak your sins forgiven :
His righteousness the only price
  That thou canst pay for heaven.

Thus God is yours—thus reconciled,
  His love your bliss secures,
The Father looks upon the child
  And saith. " All things are yours."

Efficacy of Prayer.

"When I called upon thee thou heardest me, and enduedst my soul with much strength."—PSALM ciii, 3.

WHEN troubles, wave on wave, assailed,
    And fear my soul appalled,
I knew the Lord would rescue me,
    And for deliverance called.

Still onward, onward came the flood ;
    Again I sought the Lord,
And prayed that he the waves would still
    By his resistless word.

But still they rushing came ; again
    Arose my earnest prayer,
And then I prayed for faith and strength
    Whate'er he willed, to bear.

Then his felt presence was my strength,
　　His outstretched arm was nigh ;
My head he raised, my heart he cheered,
　　" Fear not," he said, " 'tis I."

Strong in that strength, I rose above
　　The tempest's fierce alarms ;
It drove me to a port of peace,
　　Within a Saviour's arms.

Life.

If life's pleasures cheer thee,
  Give them not thy heart,
Lest the gifts ensnare thee
  From thy God to part :
His praises speak, his favor seek,
  Fix there thy hopes' foundation ;
Love him, and he shall ever be
  The rock of thy salvation.

If sorrow e'er befall thee,
  Painful though it be,
Let not fear appal thee :
  To thy Saviour flee :
16

He, ever near, thy prayer will hear,
And calm thy perturbation ;
The waves of woe shall ne'er o'erflow
The rock of thy salvation.

Death shall never harm thee,
Shrink not from his blow,
For thy God shall arm thee,
And victory bestow :
For death shall bring to thee no sting,
The grave no desolation ;
'Tis gain to die, with Jesus nigh,
The rock of thy salvation.

Hymn.

Lord, with glowing heart I'd praise thee
  For the bliss thy love bestows,
For the pardoning grace that saves me,
  And the peace that from it flows.
Help, O God! my weak endeavor,
  This dull soul to rapture raise ;
Thou must light the flame, or never
  Can my love be warmed to praise.

Praise, my soul, the God that sought thee,
  Wretched wanderer, far astray ;
Found thee lost, and kindly brought thee
  From the paths of death away.

Praise, with love's devoutest feeling,
    Him who saw thy guilt-born fear,
And, the light of hope revealing,
    Bade the blood-stained cross appear.

Lord! this bosom's ardent feeling
    Vainly would my lips express;
Low before thy foot-stool kneeling,
    Deign thy suppliant's prayer to bless.
Let thy grace, my soul's chief treasure,
    Love's pure flame within me raise;
And, since words can never measure,
    Let my life show forth thy praise.

Heaven.

"Eye hath not seen, nor ear heard, neither have entered into the heart of man, the things which God hath prepared for them that love him."—1 Cor. ii. 9.

WITH many a bright and beauteous scene
　The earth's fair bosom charms the sight,
And brighter still the gems of heaven
　Shine in the starry train of night.

Warm are the transports that the ear
　Does to the bounding heart convey,
When the bard pours the stream of song,
　And music floats the soul away.

And the mind's eye, by fancy's flight,
　Far fairer visions can behold
Than ever gladdened earthly eye,
　Or ever earthly poet told;
13*

But far above what eye, or ear,
    Or fancy's soaring flight can yield,
Shine the rich treasures of the skies,
    The glory yet to be revealed.

To tell of those high seats of bliss,
    The seraph's song imperfect proves,
Their builder is the mighty God—
    The mansions are for those he loves.

Psalm xbi.

O! bright and happy is my lot,
   And sweet the path of life to me;
All praise to thee, eternal King!
   Whose favor fixed the fair decree.

He guides me through the busy day,
   And through the long and lonely night;
Fills me with hope and holy joy,
   And guards me with his matchless might.

My mind, in all I act or plan,
   Looks to my God, and his commands ;
And, to uphold my feeble steps,
   Protector, by my side, he stands.

My heart shall beat with grateful joy,
  My ready tongue thy praise proclaim;
For thy benignant grace shall still
  Preserve and bless this mortal frame.

And thou this warm, aspiring soul,
  That breathes its humble vows to thee,
From hell's dread gloom wilt kindly save,
  And from the grave's corruption free.

Thou the bright way to heaven wilt show,
  Thy blissful courts the just receive,
Thine hand bestow celestial joys
  No tongue can tell, no heart conceive.

"Our Father who art in Heaven."

FATHER in heaven! does God who made
    And rules this universal frame—
Say, does he own a father's love,
    And answer to a father's name?

Saviour divine! cleanser of guilt,
    Redeemer of a ruined race!
These are thy cheering words, and this
    The kind assurance of thy grace.

My God! my Father! may I dare—
    I, all debased, with sin defiled—
These awful, soothing, names to join ;
    Am I thy creature and thy child ?

Art thou my Father? then no more
　My sins shall tempt me to despair;
A father pities and forgives,
　And hears a child's repentant prayer.

Art thou my Father? let me strive
　With all my powers to do thy will,
To make thy service all my care,
　And all thy kind commands fulfil.

Art thou my Father? teach my heart
　Compassion for another's woe,
And ever, to each child of thine,
　A brother's tenderness to show.

Art thou my Father? then I know
　When pain, or want, or griefs oppress,
They come but from a father's hand,
　Which wounds to heal, afflicts to bless.

Art thou my Father? then in doubt
    And darkness when I grope my way,
Thy light shall shine upon my path,
    And make my darkness like thy day.

Art thou my Father? then no more
    Tremble. my soul, at death's alarms:
He comes a messenger of love,
    To bear me to a Father's arms.

My God! my Father! I am vile,
    Prone to forget thee, weak, and blind:
Be thou my help, my strength, my trust,
    Hope of my heart! light of my mind!

Help in Trouble.

"Call upon me in the time of trouble, so will I hear thee and thou shalt praise me."—PSALM l, 50.

THY trial day on earth must bring
　　Trouble in mercy given,
To fit thee for thy conflicts here,
　　And for thy crown in heaven.

But when they come, remember then
　　A promised help is nigh;
A Father's kind and pitying ear
　　Is open to thy cry.

Then may the light of these blest words
　　On all thy pathway shine:
"I will, thou shalt;" the hearing ear
　　Be his, the praise be thine.

Man.

"The days of man are but as grass; for he flourisheth as a flower of the field.

"For as soon as the wind goeth over it, it is gone, and the place thereof shall know it no more.

"But the merciful goodness of the Lord endureth forever and ever upon them that fear him, and his righteousness upon children's children;

"Even upon such as keep his covenant and think upon his commandments to do them.

"The Lord hath prepared his seat in heaven, and his kingdom ruleth over all."—PSALM ciii.

SUCH are thy days—so shall they pass away—
As flowers that bloom at morn, at eve decay;
But then, there comes a life that knows no end—
Rich in unfading joys that far transcend
Thy highest thoughts or warmest wishes—given
To those whose days on earth have fitted them for
heaven.

16

There is a covenant—it is sealed with blood :
A risen Saviour—a forgiving God :
These all are thine ; may these thy thoughts employ,
Thy days all pass in peace, and end in joy.

July 20th, 1842.

Note to Mrs. Key.

Mrs. Key will hereby see
That Judges two or three,
And one or two more,
So as to make exactly four,
Will dine with her to-day ;
And as they cannot stay,
Four o'clock the hour must be
For dinner, and six for tea
And toast and coffee.

So saith her humble servant,
                    F. S. Key.

TRANSLATION

FROM THE

Homily of St. Chrysostom,

ON THE CHARACTER OF JOB.

Chrysostom on Job.

REMEMBER then, my brethren, in the pressure of poverty, in the pain and languor of disease, in all your afflictions, remember the sufferings of Job and blush for your complaints. But let me display to you all the terrors of a war in which all nature was combined against him.

Ten children were torn from him! all in one dreadful moment; all in the flower of life; all in the bloom of virtue! and by no ordinary means, but by a death the most cruel, the least expected. Is there any whom such a flood of ruin would not overwhelm? Any heart of adamant which could resist it? There is none; not one. For if any one of these calamities would have been of itself intolerable, think what must have been his agony against whom such a host of miseries was assembled.

Remember then, my brethren, when you have lost the cherished objects of your souls, a son, a daughter, remember, as a refuge from despair, the example of Job : look there for consolation.

Remember his words in the midst of his anguish ; they sanctify his memory with a splendor to which the lustre of a thousand diadems is pale. Behold the extent of his desolation. Behold this shipwreck of every remaining comfort, this last and bloody scene of a tragedy of horrors ! You may have wept over the grave of one child, perhaps of another, or of another; but he, of all; he, in one moment the delighted father of a numerous offspring, is, in the next, childless. Nor did they expire gradually and gently in their beds, nor did he sit by them, nor did he feel the last faint pressure of their hands, nor did he hear the dying whispers of affection. Even these sad soothings were denied him. Nor was any aggravation wanting which can add to the bitterness of grief. They died not only in youth, but in innocence, unconscious of evil, unsuspicious of misfortune. In the sons and daugh-

ters of Job he had watched every bud of virtue as
it opened; they shone in all the varieties of human
excellence, they were worthy of all his love, and
they were all beloved. If any one of these cir-
cumstances would have swelled the torrent of ad-
versity, what must have been its fury when they
were all seen united, when they all rushed together
against him? The enemy of the world had put
forth all his strength, had attacked him with all the
malignity of his nature; he had bereaved him of all
his enjoyments, he had left him no hope but for
death. When we think how these things were
borne, my brethren, we are lost in amazement, we
behold a miracle of the Almighty! The storm had
howled among his branches, had stripped him at
once of all his fruit; it had passed over him, and he
stood a leafless trunk; but he stood. The angry
waves of affliction had rolled upon him, but his bark
still floated in a sea of sorrow. All the foundations
of his faith were undermined, but the tower was
unshaken. In the intervals of pain, when disease
had suspended her tortures, that the severer tortures

of reflection might be inflicted, what must have been his feelings? His thoughts flew back to the children he had lost: sad recollection to a father! He remembered also their filial tenderness, their obedience, their endearing qualities, which had increased the natural affection of a parent, and now aggravated his misfortune. Had they been vicious, the unworthiness of their lives would have been some consolation for their loss; but the memory of their virtues showed him the inestimable value of blessings snatched from him forever. He remembered also, that, alas! he had lost all; that not one was spared; that he had no earthly object of his love remaining. Had only one survived, how would he have cherished it! how sweet would have been such a comforter in his misery! But where now was a wretched father, deprived of all his children, to look for comfort? He remembered also the suddenness of their fate. The force of grief, as of joy, is strengthened by being unexpected. How often, when death has seized upon his victim, after a few days' illness, do we hear complaints of the cruelty

of death ? Yet he had beheld the destruction of all
his children, not in a few days, nor in a few hours,
nor in one, but in a moment. In a moment the scene
of their social festivity was made a den of slaughter;
their habitation, their tomb ! At this funeral pile,
my brethren, behold a father ! He searches
among the ruins; he grasps a broken pillar of the
building; it is wet with the blood of his children.
With one trembling hand he removes a stone—the
other shrinks from the mangled limb of a child.
Their mutilated bodies are before him. The illu-
sions of hope are vanished. There is neither life,
nor form, nor feature remaining.

In vain does he attempt to recognize their well-
known lineaments, in vain to distinguish one from
another. They are all alike—all lacerated with
innumerable wounds—all crushed into a loathsome
mass of deformity.

You are agitated, my brethren ! I behold your
tears. If you cannot hear those things, how would
you have borne them ? If your hearts can be thus
melted by a cold recital of another's calamity, think

what must have been the agony of the man who beheld it, of the father who endured it!

Amid the wailings of distress, do you hear the voice of upbraiding? Does he say, Wherefore is this evil come upon me? Is this the reward of my benevolence? Have I opened my doors to the stranger? Have I distributed my wealth to the poor? Have I been a father to the fatherless? and is it therefore that I am naked and destitute? Have I instructed· my children in wisdom? Have I led them in the paths of righteousness? Have I taught them to worship God? And is it therefore that he has destroyed them? No such murmurs escape him. He kisses the hand that chastens him. He bends with resignation to the will of heaven. "The Lord gave and the Lord hath taken away, blessed be the name of the Lord." Wonder not, my brethren, that he tore his hair, that he scattered the fragments of his garments to the winds; that he fell upon the earth; that he rolled in the dust. He was a father. Had he been unmoved, his fortitude would have been without merit—a cold and brutish philosophy would have disgraced the character of Job.

MR. KEY'S SPEECH

AT A POLITICAL MEETING.

At a Political Meeting.

AFTER the regular toasts had been disposed of—the newspaper says—the following sentiment was offered by the company :

" FRANCIS S. KEY—A friend of the administration, and an incorruptible patriot; worthy of being honored, wherever genius is admired or liberty cherished, as the author of 'The Star Spangled Banner.' "

After it was drank, and the applause which it elicited, had subsided,

Mr. Key rose and expressed his thanks for the very flattering notice the company had been pleased to take of him. He never had forgotten, he said, and never should forget, that he was a native of the county whose citizens were now assembled upon an occasion so gratifying to his feelings. Though no longer a resident, its people and its scenes had never ceased to be dear to him. His annual visits here had been always anticipated with pleasure, and never, even from his boyhood, had he come within the view of these mountains, without having his warmest affections awakened at the sight. What he felt now in accepting the invitation with which he had been honored, he should not attempt to express.

The company had been pleased to declare their approbation of his song. Praise to a poet could not be otherwise than acceptable ; but it was peculiarly gratifying to him, to know, that. in obeying the impulse of his own feelings, he had awakened theirs. The song, he knew, came from the heart, and if it had made its way to the hearts of men, whose devotion to their country and to the great cause of freedom, he so well knew, he could not pretend to be insensible to such a compliment. They had recalled to his recollection the circumstances under which he had been impelled to this effort. He had seen the flag of his country waving over a city, the strength and pride of his native State—a city devoted to plunder and desolation by its assailants. He witnessed the preparation for its assault, and saw the array of its enemies as they advanced to the attack. He heard the sound of battle; the noise of the conflict fell upon his listening ear, and told him, that "the brave and the free," had met the invaders. Then did he remember that Maryland had called her sons to the defence of that flag, and that they were the sons of sires who had left their crimson foot-prints on the snows of the North, and poured out the blood of patriots, like water, on the sands of the South. Then did he remember that there was gathered around that banner, among its defenders, men who had heard and answered the call of their county, from these mountain sides, from this beautiful valley, and from this fair city of his native country; and though he walked upon a deck surrounded by a hostile fleet, detained as a prisoner, yet was his step firm, and his heart strong, as these recollections came upon him. Through the clouds of war, the stars of that banner still shone in his view, and he saw the discomfited host of its

17*

assailants driven back in ignominy to their ships. Then, in that hour of deliverance, and joyful triumph, the heart spoke; and, Does not such a country, and such defenders of their country, deserve a song? was its question. With it came an inspiration not to be resisted; and if it had been a hanging matter to make a song he must have made it. Let the praise, then, if any be due, be given, not to him, who only did what he could not help doing; not to the writer, but to the inspirers of the song. He would advert, he said, briefly, to another and still more glorious triumph. To another of our cities assailed by the same army. Before New Orleans, was the flower of the British army, the veteran conquerors of Europe; men who had broken through hosts of disciplined warriors, and the proudest walls that military science could erect. With what scorn must they have looked upon our cotton ramparts and rude militia? And the general who was to oppose, with such forces as these, their skillful and experienced leaders, what would they think of him? They thought of him, no doubt, as his present opponents still profess to think of him, as an ignorant and rash man, unfit for any command.

Yes, he continued, even now, when he has administered the government with unexampled wisdom and success, we are told that he is a man of no learning, of no ability as a writer or a speaker— and the most contemptuous comparisons are made between his qualifications and those of his rivals.

Against such a leader, and such forces, the proud host of the enemy came on. Where are now the great orators and writers? " Ubi nunc facundus Ulysses?" Where shall we find a man to disperse the advancing foes with the eloquence of a proclamation, or overwhelm them with the terrors of a speech? Andrew Jackson was there. He made neither proclamation nor speech; but he · put a tongue into the mouths of his guns, and bade them speak to them. There was a speech to be had in everlasting remembrance. It was a moving speech. It is written on the brightest page of our country's history, and future conquerors who may desire to

send their myrmidons to shores defended by free-
men, will be wise enough to remember it.

He was not disposed, he said, to undervalue those
talents in which it was said, upon what authority
he knew not, that General Jackson was so inferior
to the favorites of his opponents. The speaker and
the writer may render essential services to a coun-
try, but there are times which will demand doers
instead of talkers; and every friend of his country
has rejoiced that we had the right sort of talent at
the defence of New Orleans.

If their services were even equal, all must admit
that there was some difference in suffering and sac-
rifice between the talker and the doer, between him
who on soft carpets and to smiling audiences makes
speeches for his country, and him whose nights are
spent in sleepless vigilance and his days in toil and
peril; who offers ease, and health, and life, upon the
altars of patriotism. If there was any suffering
in speech-making, certain patriots, whose daily la-
bors in that way throughout the last winter had
been so extraordinary, were greatly to be commis-

erated. For himself, he said, that when he had a good subject, as he now had, and saw before him such a company as he now did, and read in their kindling countenances, the warm feelings of approving hearts, he considered it a pleasure and a privilege to make a speech.

But he would return to the song; the company had thought it worthy the honor of a toast. Perhaps they were not unreasonable in placing so high an estimate upon a song. It had been said by one, thought wise in the knowledge of human nature, that "if he could be allowed to make a nation's songs, he cared not who made its laws."

He would undertake to say, that if a nation's songs were of any importance to it, there was but one way of providing a supply of them. He had adverted to the occasions of which he had spoken, for the purpose of showing that way. If national poets. who shall keep alive the sacred fire of patriotism in the hearts of the people, are desirable to a country, the country must deserve them ; must put forth her patriots and heroes, whose deeds alone can furnish the necessary inspiration; when a country is thus worthy of the lyre, she will command its highest efforts.

But if ever forgetful of her past and present glory, she shall cease to be "the land of the free and the home of the brave," and become the purchased possession of a company of stock-jobbers and speculators; if her people are to become the vassals of a great moneyed corporation, and to bow down to her pensioned and privileged nobility; if the patriots who shall dare to arraign her corruptions and denounce her usurpation, are to be sacrificed upon her gilded altar; such a country may furnish venal orators and presses, but the soul of national poetry will be gone. That muse will "never bow the knee in Mammon's fane." No, the patriots of such a land must hide their shame in her deepest forests, and her bards must hang their harps upon the willows. Such a people, thus corrupted and degraded

> "Living, shall forfeit fair renown,
> And, doubly dying, shall go down
> To the vile dust from whence they sprung,
> Unwept, unhonored, and unsung."

He again thanked the company for the honor they had done him; but he could only take his share of it. He was but the instrument in executing what they had been pleased to praise; it was dictated and inspired by the gallantry and patriotism of the sons of Maryland. The honor was due, not to him who made the song, but to the heroism of those who made him make it.

He would therefore propose as a toast, the real authors of the song,

"THE DEFENDERS OF THE STAR SPANGLED BANNER: What they would not strike to a foe, they will never sell to traitors."

BOOKS

PUBLISHED BY

Robert Carter & Brothers,

285 BROADWAY,

NEW YORK.

—————◆ ○ ◆ ○ ◆—————

ABERCROMBIE'S Contest and the Armor. 32mo, gilt........	25
ADAMS' Three Divine Sisters—Faith, Hope and Charity......	50
ADVICE to a Young Christian. 18mo......................	30
ALLEINE'S Gospel Promises. 18mo.......................	30
ALEXANDER'S Counsels to the Young. 32mo, gilt..........	25
ANCIENT History of the Egyptians, Assyrians, &c. 2 vols....	2 00
ANDERSON'S Annals of the English Bible. 8vo.............	1 75
———— Family Book. 12mo.................................	75
ANLEY'S Earlswood. A Tale.............................	75
ASHTON Cottage; or, The True Faith. Illustrated..........	60
AUSTRALIA—The Loss of the Brig by Fire. 18mo..........	25
BAGSTER—The Authenticity and Inspiration of the Bible....	60
BALLANTYNE'S Mabel Grant. A Highland Story..........	50
BAXTER'S Saint's Rest. Unabridged. 8vo..................	2 00
———— Call to the Unconverted. 18mo......................	30
BIBLE Companion. Edited by Dr. Tyng.................	40
BIBLE Expositor. Illustrated. 18mo......................	50
BICKERSTETH'S Treatise on Prayer. 18mo...............	40
———— Treatise on the Lord's Supper. 18mo..................	30
———— (E. H.) Waters from the Well Spring. 16mo...........	60
BLOSSOMS of Childhood. 18mo...........................	50
BLUNT'S Coincidences, and Paley's Horæ Paulinæ. 8vo.....	2 00
BOGATSKY'S Golden Treasury. 24mo, gilt.................	50
BOLTON'S Call to the Lambs. Illustrated..................	50
———— Tender Grass for Little Lambs.......................	50
BONAR'S (Rev. Horatius) Night of Weeping.................	30
———— Morning of Joy. A Sequel to the above..............	40
———— Story of Grace......................................	30
———— Truth and Error. 18mo.............................	40
———— Man, his Religion and his World.....................	40
———— Eternal Day..	50

BONAR'S (Rev. Andrew) Commentary on Leviticus. 8vo... 1 50
BONNET'S Family of Bethany. 18mo........................ 40
—— Meditations on the Lord's Prayer. 18mo.............. 40
BOOTH'S Reign of Grace. 12mo........................... 75
BORROW'S Bible and Gypsies of Spain. 8vo, cloth......... 1 00
BOSTON'S (Thomas) Select Works. Royal 8vo.............. 2 00
—— Four-fold State. 18mo............................... 50
—— Crook in the Lot. 18mo............................. 30
BRETT'S (Rev. W. H.) Indian Tribes of Guiana. 18mo....... 50
BREWSTER'S More Worlds than One...................... 60
BRIDGEMAN'S Daughter of China. 18mo.................. 50
BRIDGES on the Christian Ministry. 8vo................. 1 50
—— on the Proverbs. 8vo............................... 2 00
—— on the CXIXth Psalm. 8vo.......................... 1 00
—— Memoir of Mary Jane Graham. 8vo........ .... 1 00
BROKEN Bud; or, the Reminiscences of a Bereaved Mother. 75
BROTHER and Sister; or, the Way of Peace................ 50
BROWN'S (Rev. John, D.D.) Exposition of First Peter. 8vo.. 2 50
—— on the Sayings and Discourses of Christ. 2 vols. 8vo.. 4 00
—— on the Sufferings and Glories of the Messiah. 8vo...... 1 50
—— The Dead in Christ. 16mo........................... 50
BROWN'S Explication of the Assembly's Catechism. 12mo.. 60
BROWN (Rev. David) on the Second Advent. 12mo.......... 1 25
BROWN'S Concordance. 32mo, gilt, 30 cents. Plain......... 20
BUCHANAN'S Comfort in Affliction. 18mo................. 40
—— on the Holy Spirit. 18mo............................ 50
BUNBURY'S Glory, Glory, Glory, and other Narratives...... 25
BUNYAN'S Pilgrim's Progress. Fine ed. Large type. 12mo. 1 00
—— 18mo. Close type................................... 50
—— Jerusalem Sinner Saved. 18mo...................... 50
—— Greatness of the Soul. 18mo........................ 50
BURNS' (John) Christian Fragments. 18mo................ 40
BUTLER'S (Bishop) Complete Works. 8vo................. 1 50
—— Sermons, alone. 8vo................................ 1 00
—— Analogy, alone. 8vo................................ 75
—— and Wilson's Analogy. 8vo.......................... 1 25
CALVIN, The Life and Times of John Calvin. By Henry.... 2 00
CAMERON'S (Mrs.) Farmer's Daughter. Illustrated......... 30
CATECHISMS—The Assembly's Catechism. Per hundred.... 1 25
—— Do. with proofs....................   "   " 3 00
—— Brown's Short Catechism....... ......   "   " 1 25
—— Brown on the Assembly's Catechism. Each............ 10
—— Willison's Communicant's Catechism. Per dozen....... 75
CECIL'S Works. 3 vols. 12mo, with portrait............... 3 00
—— Sermons, separate.................................. 1 00

CARTERS' PUBLICATIONS. 3

DAVIDSON'S Connection of Sacred and Profane History				1 00
DAVID'S Psalms, in meter. Large type. 12mo. Embossed..				75
Do.	do.	do.	gilt edges	1 00
Do.	do.	do.	Turkey morocco	2 00
Do.	18mo.	Good type.	Plain sheep	33
Do.	48mo.	Very neat pocket edition. Sheep		20
Do.	"	"	" morocco	25
Do.	"	"	" gilt edges..	31
Do.	"	"	" tucks	50
Do.	with Brown's Notes. 18mo			50
Do.	"	"	" morocco, gilt	1 25

DAVIES' Sermons. 3 vols. 12mo... 2 00
DICK'S (John, D.D.) Lectures on Theology. 2 vols. in 1. Cloth 2 50
   Do.   do.   do.   Sheep, $3. 2 vols. Cloth... 3 00
—— Lectures on Acts. 8vo... 1 50
DICKINSON'S (Rev. R. W.) Scenes from Sacred History... 1 00
—— Responses from Sacred Oracles... 1 00
DILL'S Ireland's Miseries, their Cause and Cure... 75
DODDRIDGE'S Rise and Progress. 18mo... 40
—— Life of Colonel Gardiner. 18mo... 30
DRUMMOND'S (Mrs.) Emily Vernon. A Tale. 16mo... 75
—— (Rev. D. T. K.) on the Parables. 8vo...
DUNCAN'S (Rev. Dr.) Sacred Philosophy of the Seasons. 2 vols. 2 50
—— Life, by his Son. With portrait. 12mo... 75
—— Tales of the Scottish Peasantry. 18mo. Illustrated.... 50
—— Cottage Fireside. 18mo. Illustrated... 40
—— (Mrs.) Life of Mary Lundie Duncan. 16mo... 75
—— —— Life of George A. Lundie. 18mo... 50
—— —— Memoir of George B. Phillips. 18mo... 25
—— —— Children of the Manse... 50
—— —— America as I Found It... 1 00
—— (Mary Lundie) Rhymes for my Children. Illustrated.... 25
EDWARD'S (Jonathan, D.D.) Charity and its Fruits. 18mo... 50
ENGLISH Pulpit (The). 8vo... 1 50
ERSKINE'S Gospel Sonnets. 18mo. Portrait... 50
EVENING Hours with my Children. Colored, $1 75. Plain.. 1 25
EVIDENCES of Christianity—University of Virginia. 8vo.... 2 50
FAMILY Worship. 8vo. Morocco, $5. Half calf, $4. Cloth 3 00
FANNY and her Mamma. Square... 50
FISK'S Memorial of the Holy Land, with steel plates... 1 00
—— Orphan Tale... 25
FLEETWOOD'S History of the Bible. Illustrated... 2 00
FLORENCE Egerton; or, Sunshine and Shadow. Illustrated. 75
FOLLOW Jesus. By the author of "Come to Jesus"... 25
FORD'S Decapolis. 18mo... 25

HISTORY of the Puritans and Pilgrim Fathers. 12mo........ 1 00
HISTORY of the Reformation in Europe. 18mo.............. 40
HOOKER (Rev. H.), The Uses of Adversity. 18mo............ 30
———— Philosophy of Unbelief. 12mo...................... 75
HORNE'S Introduction. 2 vols. Royal 8vo. Half cloth...... 3 50
    Do.   1 vol., sheep, $4. 2 vols., sheep, $5. 2 vols., cloth. 4 00
HORNE'S (Bishop) Commentary on the Book of Psalms. 8vo. 1 50
HOWARD (John); or, the Prison World of Europe. 16mo.... 75
HOWELL'S Life—Perfect Peace. 18mo...................... 30
HOWE'S Redeemer's Tears. 18mo.......................... 50
HOWIE'S Scots Worthies. 8vo............................ 1 50
HUSS (John) Life of. Translated from the German... 25
INFANT'S Progress. 18mo. Illustrated.................... 50
JACOBUS on Matthew. With a Harmony. Illustrated....... 75
———— on Mark and Luke................................. 75
———— on John and Acts (preparing)..................... 75
———— Catechetical Questions on each vol. Per dozen.......... 1 50
JAMES' Anxious Inquirer. 18mo............................ 30
———— Christian Progress. 18mo.......................... 30
———— True Christian. 18mo.............................. 30
———— Widow Directed. 18mo............................ 30
———— Young Man from Home. 18mo...................... 30
———— Christian Professor. 16mo......................... 75
———— Christian Duty. 16mo............................. 75
———— Christian Father's Present. 16mo.................. 75
———— Course of Faith. 16mo............................ 75
———— Young Woman's Friend. 16mo..................... 75
———— Young Man's Friend. 16mo........................ 75
JAMIE Gordon; or, the Orphan. Illustrated. 18mo.......... 50
JANEWAY'S Heaven upon Earth. 18mo.................... 50
———— Token for Children. 18mo......................... 50
JAY'S Morning and Evening Exercises. Large type. 4 vols.. 4 00
    Do.   do.   Cheap edition. 2 vols........ 1 50
———— Autobiography and Reminiscences. 2 vols. 12mo..... 2 50
———— Female Scripture Characters. 12mo.................. 1 00
———— Christian Contemplated. 18mo...................... 40
JEANIE Morrison; or, the Discipline of Life. 16mo.......... 75
              By the same Author.
    A New Volume, uniform with the above.............. 75
    THE Pastor's Family. 18mo......................... 25
JOHNSON'S Rasselas. Elegant edition. 16mo.............. 50
KENNEDY'S (Grace) Profession is not Principle. 18mo...... 30
———— Father Clement. 18mo............................. 30
———— Anna Ross. 18mo. Illustrated...................... 30
———— Philip Colville. A Covenanter's Story.............. 30

MORE'S (Hannah) Private Devotion. 18mo................... 30
   Do.   do.   do.   32mo. 20 cents. Gilt... 80
MORELL'S History of Modern Philosophy. 8vo.............. 3 00
MORNING of Life. 18mo............................ 40
MORNING and Night Watches............................ 60

By the same Author :—
   FOOTSTEPS of St. Paul. 12mo. Illustrated........... 1 00
   FAMILY Prayers. 12mo.............................. 75
   WOOD-CUTTER of Lebanon, and Exiles of Lucerna.... 50
   THE Great Journey. Illustrated...................... 50
   THE Words of Jesus................................. 40
   THE Mind of Jesus................................. 40
MY School-Boy Days. 18mo. Illustrated.................... 30
MY Youthful Companions. 18mo Illustrated................ 30
   The above two in one volume........................ 50
NEW Cobwebs to Catch Little Flies........................ 50
NEWTON'S (Rev. John) Works. 2 vols. in 1. Portrait....... 2 00
NOEL'S Infant Piety. 18mo................................ 25
OBERLIN (John Frederick) Memoirs of...................... 40
OLD White Meeting-House. 18mo........................... 40
OLD Humphrey's Observations — Addresses — Thoughts for
   Thoughtful—Walks in London—Homely Hints—Country
   Strolls—Old Sea Captain—Grand parents—Isle of Wight—
   Pithy Papers—Pleasant Tales—North American Indians.
   12 vols. 18mo. Each................................ 40
OPIE on Lying. New edition. 18mo. Illustrated........... 40
OSBORNE (Mrs.) The World of Waters. Illustrated. 18mo... 50
OWEN on Spiritual Mindedness. 12mo...................... 60
PALEY'S Evidences. Edited by Prof. Nairne................ 1 25
   ——— Horæ Paulinæ. 8vo................................... 75
PASCAL (Jaqueline); or, Convent Life in Port Royal. 12mo.. 1 00
   ——— Provincial Letters................................. 1 00
PASTOR'S Daughter. By Louisa Payson Hopkins............ 40
PATTERSON on the Assembly's Shorter Catechism.......... 50
PEARSON on Infidelity. Fine edition. 8vo. $2. Cheap ed... 60
PEEP of Day.. 30

By the same Author :—
   LINE upon Line..................................... 30
   PRECEPT on Precept................................. 30
   NEAR Home... 50
   FAR Off.. 50
   SCRIPTURE Facts.................................... 50
PHILIP'S Devotional Guides. 2 vols...................... 1 50
   ——— Young Man's Closet Library...................... 75

CARTERS' PUBLICATIONS.

9

PHILIP'S Mary's, Martha's, Lydia's and Hannah's Love of the Spirit. Each 40
PIKE'S True Happiness. 18mo 30
—— Divine Origin of Christianity 30
POLLOK'S Course of Time. Elegant edition. 16mo. Portrait 1 00
—— Do. 18mo. Small copy. Close type 40
—— Life, Letters and Remains. By the Rev. J. Scott, D.D... 1 00
—— Tales of the Scottish Covenanters. Illustrated 50
—— Helen of the Glen. 18mo. Illustrated 25
—— Persecuted Family   "   "   25
—— Ralph Germnell   "   "   25
POOL'S Annotations. 3 vols. 8vo. Half calf, $12. Cloth.... 10 00
PRAYERS of St. Paul. 16mo 75
QUARLE'S Emblems. Illustrated 1 00
RETROSPECT (The). By Aliquis. 18mo 40
RICHMOND'S Domestic Portraiture. Illustrated. 16mo..... 75
—— Annals of the Poor. 18mo 40
RIDGELY'S Body of Divinity. 2 vols. Royal 8vo 4 00
ROGER Miller; or, Heroism in Humble Life. 18mo 30
ROGER'S Jacob's Well. 18mo 40
—— Folded Lamb. 18mo 40
ROMAINE on Faith. 12mo 60
—— Letters. 12mo 60
RUTHERFORD'S Letters. With Life by Bonar 1 50
RYLE'S Living or Dead. A Series of Home Truths 75
—— Wheat or Chaff 75
—— Startling Questions 75
—— Rich and Poor 75
—— Priest, Puritan and Preacher 75
SAPHIR (Philip) Life of 30
SCHMID'S Hundred Short Tales 50
SCOTIA'S Bards. A Collection of the Scottish Poets 2 00
SCOTT'S Daniel. A Model for Young Men 1 50
—— (Thos.) Force of Truth. 18mo 25
SELECT Works of James Venn, Wilson, Philip and Jay 1 50
—— Christian Authors. 2 vols. 8vo 2 00
SELF Explanatory Bible. Half calf, $4 50. Morocco 6 00
SERLE'S Christian Remembrancer 50
SHERWOOD'S Clever Stories. Square 50
—— Jack the Sailor Boy 25
—— Duty is Safety 25
—— Think before you Act 25
SINNER'S Friend. 18mo 25
SIGOURNEY'S (Mrs. L. H.) Water Drops. Illust. 16mo...... 75
—— Letters to my Pupils. With portrait. 16mo 75

SIGOURNEY'S Memoir of Mrs. L. H. Cook...................   75
——— Olive Leaves..   50
——— Faded Hope...   50
——— Boy's Book. 18mo....................................   40
——— Girl's Book. 18mo....................................   40
——— Child's Book. Square..................................   35
SINCLAIR'S Modern Accomplishments.....................   75
——— Modern Society...   75
——— Hill and Valley..   75
——— Holyday House...   50
——— Charlie Seymour......................................   30
SMITH'S (Rev. James) Green Pastures for the Lord's Flock...   1 00
SMYTH'S Bereaved Parents Consoled. 12mo...............   75
SONGS in the House of my Pilgrimage. 18mo.   75
SORROWING yet Rejoicing..................................   30
STEVENSON'S Christ on the Cross. 12mo...................   75
——— Lord our Shepherd. 12mo............................   60
——— Gratitude. 12mo......................................   75
STORIES on the Lord's Prayer..............................   30
STUCKLEY'S Gospel Glass..................................   75
SUMNER'S Exposition of Matthew and Mark. 12mo.........   75
SYMINGTON on Atonement. 12mo.........................   75
TALES from English History. Illustrated....................   75
TAYLOR'S (Jane) Hymns for Infant Minds. Square. Illust...   40
——— Rhymes for the Nursey. Square. Illustrated..........   50
——— Limed Twigs to Catch Young Birds. Square. Illust...   50
——— Life and Correspondence. 18mo.....................   40
——— Display. A Tale. 18mo.............................   30
——— Original Poems and Poetical Remains. Illustrated.....   40
——— (Isaac) Loyola; or, Jesuitism in its Rudiments..........   1 00
——— ——— Natural History of Enthusiasm................   75
——— (Jeremy) Sermons. Complete in 1 vol. 8vo............   1 50
TENNENT'S Life...   25
THEOLOGICAL Sketch Book. 2 vols................ ....   3 00
THREE Months under the Snow. 18mo.....................   30
THORNWELL'S Discourses on Truth.......................   1 00
TUCKER, The Rainbow in the North. 18mo...   50
——— Abbeokuta or, Sunrise in the Tropics. 18mo..........   50
——— The Southern Cross and the Southern Crown..........   75
TURNBULLS Genius of Scotland. Illustrated. 16mo.......   1 00
——— Pulpit Orators of France and Switzerland.... ....   1 00
TYNG'S Lectures on the Law and Gospel. With portrait.....   1 50
——— Christ is All. 8vo. With portrait...................   1 50
——— Israel of God. 8vo. Enlarged edition.................   1 50
——— Rich Kinsman..   1 00

———◆◆———

BOOKS NOT STEREOTYPED.

HOWELL'S Remains.. 75
LONDON Lectures to Young Men, 1853-4.................... 1 00
"   "   1854-5..................... 1 00
MALAN'S Pictures from Switzerland......................... 60
OWEN'S Works. 16 vols. 8vo.............................. 20 00
PRATT (Josiah) Memoirs of................................. 1 50
SMITH'S (Jno. Pye) Scripture Testimony to Messiah.......... 5 00
SELF-EXPLANATORY Bible, half calf, $4,50 mor............ 6 00
SWETE'S Family Prayers..................................... 60
THOLUCK'S Hours of Devotion............................. 60
VILLAGE Churchyard. 18mo.............................. 40
——— Pastor. 18mo..................................... 40
——— Observer. 18mo...................................... 30
WILSON (Prof.), The Forester, a Tale....................... 75
WORDS to Win Souls. 12mo................................ 75

THE FIRESIDE SERIES.

A Series of beautiful volumes of the Narrative kind, uniform in bind-
ing, and prettily Illustrated. 18mo. Price 50 cents each.

The following are now ready:

MABEL GRANT. A Highland Story.
THE WOODCUTTER OF LEBANON.
LOUIS AND FRANK.
CLARA STANLEY. A Story for Girls.
THE CLAREMONT TALES.
THE CONVENT. By Miss M'Crindell.
FAR OFF. By the author of the "Peep of Day."
NEAR HOME. By the same author.
HAPPY HOME. By Dr. Hamilton.
JAMIE GORDON; or, the Orphan.
THE CHILDREN OF THE MANSE. By Mrs. Duncan.
TALES OF THE SCOTTISH PEASANTRY.
SCHOOL DAYS AND COMPANIONS.
THE INDIAN TRIBES OF GUIANA.
HOLIDAY HOUSE. By Miss Sinclair.
OLIVE LEAVES. By Mrs. Sigourney.
BROTHER AND SISTER.
POLLOK'S TALES OF THE COVENANTERS.
THE RAINBOW IN THE NORTH.
THE INFANT'S PROGRESS. By Mrs. Sherwood.
THE WORLD OF WATERS.
BLOSSOMS OF CHILDHOOD.
MAY DUNDAS. A Tale.
ABBEOKUTA; or, Sunrise in the Tropics.
THE FAMILY AT HEATHERDALE.